What They Don't Teach You at Film School

▸▸WHAT THEY DON'T TEACH YOU AT FILM SCHOOL◂◂

161 Strategies for Making Your Own Movie No Matter What

Camille Landau
and
Tiare White

New York

Library of Congress Cataloging-in-Publication Data

Landau, Camille.
    What they don't teach you at film school / by Camille Landau and Tiare White.—1st ed.
        p.   cm.
    ISBN 0-7868-8477-0
    1. Motion pictures—Production and direction. I. White, Tiare. II. Title.
PN1995.9.P7 L28   2000
791.43'0232—dc21   00-022214

First Edition

10   9   8

CONTENTS

THE CREDITS

The credits of student films run hysterically long, with the wonderful, generous people who gave in love, kindness, favors, and friendship. So do ours. Like a film, this book couldn't have happened without any one of them playing the following roles and, of course, much more.

LOVE
Babette, Bob, Florence, George, Julien, Kevin, Mervy, and Scott.

FAITH
Betsy Amster, David Cashion, and Alison Lowenstein.

FRIENDSHIP
Reed, Lisa, Daria, David, Jennifer, Preedar, Adam, Frank, Moses, Maurie, Mary, Dean, Gavin, Carmen, Sylvie, Christine, Yasuko, Carla, Jen, Susan, Benjamin, Dan, Ticky, Nick, Lara, Skye, Eddie, Lucy, Mark, Joseph, Phillip, Amy, Fawn, Micha, Jason, Randy, Thorbjorn, Elizabeth, Patrick, Wei-Shan, Laurie, Riccardo, Cecily, Brenda, Hal, Tina, John, Niki, Linda, Aleen, Kit, Natalie, Deanna, Rachael, Arthur, Larry, Tommy, Justin, Thomas, Beth, Andrew and Stacie, Karen, and Shelley.

TEACHERS IN THE TRUEST SENSE
Paul Fawcett, Robb Moss, Paul Lucey, Amanda Pope, Marie Barnett, Allison Humenuk, Philip Gordis, David McFadden, Sylvia Jones, Seamus Heaney, Frank Frattaroli.

GUIDANCE

Amedeo D'Adamo, Kim Adelman, Darren Aronofsky, Levi Asher,
James Bacon, Reed Bernstien, Anne Boron, Peter Broderick,
Dan Budsen, Luis Camara Silva, Todd Cherniowsky, Maxie Collier,
Adam Collis, Julia Comege, Andrew Crane, Dan Cutrara,
David Davidson, Tamra Davis, Amy Dawes, Scott Derrickson,
Mel Donaldson, Carmen Elly, Kevin Fitzgerald, Gabriel Friedman,
Chris Eyre, Reena Farul, Chuck Fries, Charlie Grant, Larry Greenburg,
James Gunn, Tom Hadley, Jennifer Haskin-O'Reggio, Gregory Gardener,
Jon Gerrans, Brian Hecker, Cyrus Helf, Gill Holland, Dean Hollander,
Lewis Horwitz, Marcus Hu, Lew Hunter, Andrew Hurwitz,
Lindsay Jewett, Karen Johnson, Carey Jones, Lloyd Kaufman,
Patrick Keating, Val Keller, Tom Kelly, Aleen Keshishian, Laura Kim,
Greg Laemmle, Reeves Lehman, Philip Levens, Louise Levison, Emanuel
Levy, Barney Lichtenstein, Frank Maddalone, Liz Manne,
Karo Martesko, Matt McDowell, Larry Meistrich, Tom Miller,
Velko Milosevich, Dan Mirvish, Kathy Morgan, Thom Mount,
Donie Nelson, Jeremiah Newton, Vaughn Obern, Dennis O'Connor,
Mobilaje Olambiwonnu, Laura Pak, Carolyn Pfeiffer, John Pierson,
Gavin Pollack, Thierry Pathe, Rod Plummer, Pliny Porter, Pat Quinn,
Roger Raderman, Brooks Rawlins, Steve Rodriguez, Cecily Rhett,
Somi Roy, David Russell, Dan Sanford, Susan Seidelman, Garo Setian,
Laurie Shearing, Lisa Singer, Michael Shuken, Mary Jane Skalski,
Bradley Spann, Tom Stempel, Amy Taubin, Harry Tulchin,
Eric Vaterlaus, Amy Wadell, Bob Ware, Shelley Wenk, Kennedy Wheatley,
Marilyn White, Don Zirpola.

INSPIRATION

Peter Meier, Lloyd Kaufman, Leonard Cohen, Aretha Franklin,
Penny Marshall, Pat Quinn, Jodie Foster, Pats and Eds.

KINDNESS AND SUPPORT

Katie, Anders, Nora and Beatrice of the Novel; Doug, Marie, Jennifer,
Melissa, Stacy, Paula and Narcy of Korokia; Dr. Patricia Broadhead;
Dr. Robert Trafeli; Mark Trafeli; Louise, Meredith, Susan, Jackie,

*Nicole, Karen, James, and Nora of Protocare; Jean, Lee, and Jim of
Times-Mirror; Andrea of Artisan; Abby, Andrew,
and Anthony of Edgemar.*

INTEREST
*Our readers. We are grateful for your interest, and for your comments.
Please e-mail us at ima@soca.com.*

INTRODUCTION

WHAT THEY DON'T TEACH YOU—
YOU CAN MAKE FILMS IF YOU WANT TO.

INT. SCHOOL OF CINEMA-TELEVISION—MORNING, THE FIRST DAY OF CLASS

Four hundred new FILM STUDENTS turn eager faces to the senior PROFESSOR, who rises to speak.

PROFESSOR
Put up your hands if you want to direct.

Four hundred film students put up their hands.

PROFESSOR
Now everybody put them down, except for one.

Four hundred film students don't know what to do.
He pauses before the kill.

PROFESSOR
And that's if you're lucky.

Every year students commit to taking a long uphill hike on what they're told is a dead-end road to being a filmmaker. The worst part? CUT TO: four years and $80,000 later, and most believed the professor was right.

Few from the class in question finished with a film of their own. Most lost confidence that they could direct. Many even lost faith they could make films at all. Some made films anyway, despite what the teachers said they couldn't do.

What they don't teach you in film school is that you can make films if you want to. With or without film school. With or without a budget, a crew, actors, or an audience, you can make films.

More important than understanding *how* to make films is understanding *why* you want to. Clarity about your convictions and motivations will push you to start making film, even when no one has given you a green light. This is the vision that will pull you to the finish line. It's what will get you to make your next film, and the next one after that.

We want you to make film*s*, plural. We want you to make this film, and the next one, and the one after that, because film itself is your best teacher. From making films you'll learn your own answers to the "hows" and—whether or not you're ready—plenty about the "whys." Make films and you'll learn everything you haven't yet learned about yourself, including why you're doing this in the first place.

We believe that filmmaking should be hard, but not because of its technical and logistical demands. Rather, we think it should challenge you because of the pressure it does and should put on your vision of yourself, what you have to give, and what you crave to gain. The practical hints throughout this book add up to one thing: we think the mechanical details should not be allowed to hold your imagination hostage. Too much is at stake: what you want to say and why you need to say it.

1

EVERYTHING YOU NEED TO KNOW

▶▶1. DON'T ASK FOR PERMISSION.

Don't get in the habit of asking for permission, or you'll forget your own strength.

The danger with film school as the initiation to filmmaking is that so many schools are built on the very logic of permission. If they let you in, then you're a filmmaker. If they choose your project, then you're a director. If they like you, you'll succeed.

What if they don't?

Too many film students and would-be filmmakers make careers out of asking permission from people whose job it is to say no, when all they should be doing is figuring out how to make films—with or without anyone's blessing.

Only four students in each class of forty-five at one top film school get chosen to direct an advanced narrative film. The rest are required to *pay* six units to take a crew position on "the chosen's" films. After spending $4,000 to hold a boom mike on someone else's set, many students give up hope of ever directing. They trudge through the rest of their requirements without picking up a camera again.

It's needless to say, but we'll say it anyway: the selection process, by its nature, is terminally flawed. The mother-may-I system exists to protect schools' limited resources. Buying into it keeps you from complaining that there aren't more facilities, equipment, or opportunities. It turns your resentment toward the student whose project was chosen and, ultimately, against yourself.

Most schools have their own painful variation of the game.

Another top film school used to decimate its first-year class, inviting just a handful back to the second year to make a film and leave with a degree. Now, they've found a certain logic in the following scheme: all students get invited back to pay the second year's tuition, but only a few are selected to work on film. The rest continue to pay just as much tuition, only to shoot on video. At yet another top film school students pay all the expenses on their third-year films, then vie to get them screened on the night the school invites agents and producers. The films that don't make the cut barely get seen by anyone outside the directors' families.

Given the odds against being officially selected for school-sponsored projects, those who refuse to play by the rules are more likely to make films. Dan Mirvish (USC Class of '94) didn't get chosen to make one of the school-financed films, so he decided to make a thesis film on his own. Dan says that when his professors told him the film couldn't be more than twenty minutes long and still count for his degree, he made a feature in Omaha.

The story doesn't end there. When Dan's film, *Omaha (the movie)*, wasn't accepted at the Sundance Festival, he started his own festival with three friends whose films had also been rejected. They called it "Slamdance '95: Anarchy in Utah," set up their projector down the hall from a Sundance screening room, and ran their films concurrently. The very same agents, producers, and distributors came.

Slamdance is going into its sixth successful year, with over 1,700 submissions per festival, sold-out screenings, and distribution deals for a number of the films that premiered there.

Omaha (the movie) played in thirty-five cities, had a long L.A. release, and was picked up by the Sundance cable channel. Dan says that if you read closely, the station's program notes claim the film screened at Sundance. He says he knew the film would be accepted someday.

▶▶ 2. ALWAYS BE FIFTEEN.

At fifteen you don't believe in "authority." Not without question, anyway. And certainly not more than you believe in your own.

Years later, you may be wiser but not smarter. You're worried about having money, a job, etc., and for this you make some compromises to get the approval of the people who are in a position to make this happen for you. You are afraid of losing something— your nascent financial independence—and this fear nudges you into a relationship to authority figures where you give over to them a certain piece of your brilliant, untamed self in exchange for . . . some cash.

Years later, you have further to go to make a good film. You have to start by going backward, back to the spirit of sneaking into movies, telling loud jokes, thinking food fights are funny and that first love will last. Film schools, of course, will not generally support this kind of behavior. They are like finishing schools that seek to teach their willing pupils the rules of the game, the social and creative graces, and the virtues of marrying well (i.e., getting a great studio deal). The object is to turn out filmmakers who will understand where they can fit in the existing scheme of things, thereby achieving professional (if not necessarily creative) success.

Professional success is easier for them to measure than creative success. It can be measured in terms of dollars. Are you working? Are you making big bucks on films that cost big bucks? If so, you can be sure that you will be listed on every mailer your school sends out. Look, they'll say, we know how to train people. Our former students are "making it."

This is nothing to sneer at. We all want to make it one way or another, but too often filmmaker aspirants confuse "making it" with "doing it." You can have one without the other. For instance, you can be making a lot of money on a film but not doing anything that creatively charges you or makes you feel that you are fulfilling your creative destiny. You can also fulfill your creative destiny and not make a dime doing it. Both don't have to happen simultaneously.

If you compromise yourself by making films that don't engage you creatively, we really don't know why you're making them at all. And chances are, neither does your fifteen-year-old self.

▶▶ 3. YOU AREN'T PROMISED TOMORROW. MAKE TODAY'S FILM TODAY.

Camille's great aunt in Corsica buys new bread every day, yet always eats the day-old kind. Why? She starts out with too much bread, but goes to the bakery anyway. She comes home with the fresh bread, but feels bad about the old bread, so she eats that first. The simple solution would be ditching the old bread, eating the fresh, and then buying more tomorrow. She's eating yesterday's bread and missing out on today's. All while today's turns into tomorrow's yesterday's.

Filmmakers get caught in a similar trap. Instead of making, and enjoying, today's film, they think about how they're going to get tomorrow's. Going so far as to make a film they don't love in order to be in a "better" position to make the one they want to make tomorrow.

You aren't promised tomorrow, says our friend Frank Maddalone. And you aren't promised your next film. So enjoy the film you're making now, and make sure it's the one you most want to make.

▶▶ 4. THIS ISN'T THE LAST FILM YOU'LL EVER MAKE, SO MAKE THE ONE YOU CAN AFFORD.

Small is fine. The goal is to make a film and then to make another film. And another one after that.

If you want to make a film now, make the film you can make now. If you wait to make the film you want to make "eventually," you'll eventually lose interest. You'll have also lost the chance to make the film you can make today, as the person you are now.

Spend what you have to spend and no more. Also, pay attention to how much you have in your emotional budget. Just as you only have so much money, you only have so much energy and patience, and only so many best friends. Look around you. If you have a big collection of Barbie dolls but can't afford to feed—let alone pay—actors, make a film with them. Todd Haynes is as well known for the Karen Carpenter biography film he made with Barbies (*Superstar: The Karen Carpenter Story*) as for any of his bigger films (*Safe, Poison*). It's *Superstar* that got him a fan in producer Christine Vachon, who has produced his movies since.

Garo Setian was the first person in Camille's USC classes to achieve commercial success. He got it with a short film starring a lump of clay called "The Blob." It won loads of festivals, was nominated for a student Academy Award™, sold to cable, and was considered for a TV series.

Sadly, stories of first-time filmmakers spending (way) more than they can afford are a dime a . . . hundred. One friend, let's just call him Bill, didn't believe anyone's warnings against making a 35mm feature for his first film, or starting production without nearly enough money or time. Instead, he started shooting with a producer he didn't trust, a number of crucial locations still unsecured, and not enough money for developing the film as he shot it.

When he finally saw the footage (at the end of his shoot, when it was too late), he saw that the camera hadn't kept focus, or sync. From three weeks of shooting he only had one usable shot. By now he had already spent more money than he had. Still, he decided he had no choice but to spend more.

Studios are notorious for getting caught in the same sand trap—gambling more money on a film that's in a load of trouble, only to lose a load more money. But studios have a bigger safety net than you do. When they lose millions on an overblown special-effects movie, someone *might* lose their job. When Bill put $60,000 on his credit cards, he had to work endless overtime at a job he hated just to make the payments.

All this, and no happy ending. In the end, Bill netted three minutes of usable footage. He's using it to try raising (still more) money to make the longer version.

People who fling themselves at a film they can't afford either emotionally or financially find themselves eight years later still trying to complete it. Part of your skill as a filmmaker truly comes from knowing your personal, professional, creative, and financial limitations. Indeed, this knowledge may be your most valuable skill. If you know, and respect, your limitations, you'll know when you need other people's help to get to your desired destination, and you'll ask for it, in advance.

The most successful creative people are experts in defining reality. They are very good at looking objectively at the gap between what they have and what they need to actualize their vision. This is a skill you can practice and develop. It adds up to the confidence that you have the thought process to get from A to B, no matter what A or B are.

No single film has to prove or say everything you need to prove or say. You'll have a lifetime to try—one film at a time. In terms of your confidence, experience, résumé, and reel, a film is a film. Each one of them will challenge you plenty. The key is to fight dragons you know you're ready for. Because you *don't* want this to be the last film you'll ever make.

▶▶ 5. PERSISTENCE CAN TAKE YOU FAR.

M. F. McDowell graduated from UCLA film school with a feature he made as his thesis project. He thought it would hit just like *sex, lies, and videotape*. It didn't. He got a limited release in Africa. He was still in debt. He took a job picking up rocks from a golf course in Utah. His mother died. Then his wife told him that she was pregnant with another man's child.

Such a sequence of events would be enough to send most mortals spinning into existential despair, but M.F. didn't fall apart. Instead, he moved back to L.A. and went back to square one: writing scripts. When his first script, "Box," was done, he bought mailing labels of literary agents' addresses and did a mass, blind mailing of query letters. The kind of mailing they tell you never to do. He got lots of rejections. But one agent liked the letter, and liked his script. She sold it, to the producers of Academy Award–winning *Gods and Monsters*. Within a year the film, starring Billy Baldwin, was made. M.F. had the pleasure of watching its first screening, sitting next to his new wife. Then driving home in their new car. To their new house.

Success happens as the result of just one person believing in you. Make that two. You need to believe in yourself first and last. M.F. heard no enough times to understand what it meant. He just decided not to believe it.

2

THE SIGN YOU'VE BEEN SEARCHING FOR

▶▶6. THE SHORTCUT.

If you want to be a filmmaker, put down this book and pick up a camera. Any camera: Super-8, hi-8 video, or a disposable point and click still kind from the supermarket. Go and shoot a story about the kid across the street, your dog, your dying house plant . . . WHATEVER! GO DO IT NOW!

OK. Done? Now how do you feel? Exhilarated? Or like an idiot?

If you feel great, that's a good sign. If you can't wait to show your stuff, whatever its flaws, to the first breathing person in a five-foot radius, then that's even better. You are a filmmaker waiting to happen. No . . . you *are* a filmmaker.

You don't need a fancy degree or a studio deal to make you feel like you've done something significant. You are a rare bird: a self-starter. Motivated and simultaneously rewarded by the sheer plea-sure of seeing your own work. Gifted with enough self-esteem to shamelessly seek out your own audience, confident they'll love it as much as you do. You don't need this book, but we're glad to have spent this brief moment with you. Let us know when you're in town for the Oscars™.

Back to the rest of us. Probably, you were so afraid that you didn't pick up the camera at all. Afraid to feel stupid, embarrassed, or ashamed to be doing something so . . . indulgent? Clichéd? Self-absorbed? Impractical? Need we go on? Those mean bulldogs at the doors of Hollywood won't need to stop you. You won't let *yourself* out of the gate. What they don't teach you at film school is that it's not Hollywood's approval that will determine if you die feeling like a successful filmmaker. It's your own.

▶▶ 7. WHY WAIT FOR SOMETHING YOU ALREADY HAVE?

You've grown up with just two images of people who make films: the ones whose lives started with *Star Wars*, and the ones who think film ended with Godard.

You're not sure where that leaves you.

From what you've been led to believe, the *Star Wars* guys are cheerfully tuning up their SUVs, waxing up their boards, and cruising straight to USC. Just as surely, the Godard fans, with a half-pack of cigarettes and dark sunglasses, are on the road to NYU's heart of darkness.

You're still not sure where that leaves you. Except that you like film. You're not even sure if that counts. You don't have a filmmaker stereotype you identify with, no one in your family has ever made films, and sometimes you wonder where you got the idea at all.

Maybe, secretly, you're hoping to read that you don't belong. Then you could put the book down and forget all about it. You could go back to your job or your law homework, resign yourself fully, and never look back.

Sorry.

If you're reading this book, you're interested in film. As far as we know, that's the only qualification you need.

You're sure it's more complicated than that. You have at least a hundred questions to get answered before you could even think about picking up a camera. These questions are only hiding the big one: your doubt in yourself. We can answer that, too: forget it.

Doubt is a fact of most people's lives. It places you in the company of most, if not all, filmmakers. It doesn't in the least bit disqualify you. It can, in fact, help you make better films. The attention you spend on your questions about what you're doing will prompt you to make more honest choices and more original work.

Still, you might be waiting for your "sign." All we can do is point out that you're reading this book, and not *What They Don't Teach You About the CPA Exam*. If the realization that you want to make films didn't come to you as an epiphany, but as the result of a more rocky process, it doesn't make it any less valid.

What we mean to say is that you already know everything you need to know about yourself to start making movies. Filmmaking interests you now, and for the time being, you want to know more about it. Now, therefore, is when you should be making films.

▶▶8. DESIRE IS TALENT IN THE RAW.

No one's born with "filmmaker" stamped on his or her head. When you're born, you're a mystery. To your parents, to everyone. You're the latest product of the genetic lottery. No one knows what your first word will be (or your last). You don't come with an instruction manual, and no one knows what you can do. Including you.

You get to find out through trial and error, and since there are so many options, desire plays a key role. It's the only sign you have to guide you toward what you want and need; it's the magnet that pulls you toward your aspiration's true north. Following its call leads to accomplishment and, with it, what eventually gets labeled as "talent."

History's achievements started as nothing more, or less, than desires. More modestly, desire also built the bookstore you're standing in, brought you the coffee you're drinking and the book you're reading. Desire is there before anything and everything else. It's the crucial catalyst to action, and it's telling you what to do next.

Levi Asher was, and is, a computer programmer from Queens. Levi loves Dostoyevsky. One day he felt the need to make a film based on his work. He took a couple of basic production classes at a local non-degree–granting film school and bought a one-chip hi-8 camera. Every day after work he filmed his office coworkers and friends around New York, acting out the story line of *Notes from the Underground*.

Along the way Levi learned about the limitations of his camera and its built-in microphone, the limits to his actors' patience, and the limitations, at that point, of his marketing and electronic distribution knowledge. Along the way he (read: his desire) found solutions to each of these problems.

Levi shot fast motion in low-light situations, although his camera was not designed for it, to surreal and stunningly beautiful results. He placated his "actors" by shooting their scenes over drinks in the lobby of Manhattan's Royalton Hotel. He mastered computer technology that few had applied to film distribution, making his film one of the first features to be distributed online.

Levi said there is no way that he would have spent all of the time he did to put the film together unless he really loved the material and just wanted to make it into a film—any kind of film—no matter what. Desire completed his film, and made him a filmmaker and even an entrepreneur along the way. *Notes from the Underground* (the film) was reviewed in *Wired*, and, through online sales alone, has made a profit.

Your desire to make film may not come from any place as lofty as the annals of Russian literature, and that's all right. Maybe you just want to make "the grossest student film ever." With this explicit mission in mind, Cyrus Helf got on a plane from Canada and enrolled at Los Angeles Community College. He learned the filmmaking basics, went back to Canada, and cast his family in his second-year project, "Zitlover."

We met Cyrus by accident when we opened the door to the small editing room he was inhabiting at LACC. Hunched over an old flatbed, Cyrus was practically bursting with glee over the sheer "grossness" of his footage. Even if it was called "Zitlover" (or maybe *because* it was called "Zitlover"), we had to watch.

"Zitlover" didn't disappoint. It was easily the grossest student film we'd ever seen, and we loved it. Not only just for its efficient use of dialogue (the only complete line being, "Boy, sit down and eat your goddamned monkey"). Or for the brave, comic, sheer grossness of those exploding, oozing zits. It was Cyrus's uncensored joy of sharing maximum gore that seeped through the film, and it's what really got us.

"Zitlover" was immediately invited to some popular festivals, and an executive at MTV who saw it gave Cyrus an on-the-spot job offer. Cyrus will no doubt be able to pay off the money he borrowed from his parents for LACC tuition from his first paycheck, and still have enough left over to start planning his next film. Not a bad return on following your creative bliss. Wherever it leads you.

Desire is a sign. Spoken to you. Of something you already know you need to do. Talent, in contrast, is a judgment rendered after the fact. Which is why it is literally the last thing you need. You will meet up with it eventually, at the intersection between your desire and the skill that it inspires.

▶▶9. FACE THE FEAR ITSELF.

There are hundreds of excuses for not making films, but they really boil down to one: fear. Of failure, most specifically. By the transitive property of equality, we'll demonstrate:

"I'm really good at what I'm doing now" = "I'm afraid I won't be good at making films" = fear of failure.

"I tried" = "I didn't really give it my best shot" = "I'm afraid if I give it my best shot and fail, I'll really have failed" = fear of failure.

"I really tried" = "I failed and don't want to fail again" = fear of failure.

Freud wrote that fear is a wish. If he's right, then fear of failure = a wish for failure = a sign of a masochistic fantasy life. Not sure why you're wishing for failure? Here's our theory: no one knows what the future is, and it's the unknown itself that's really scary. To face it, people make wishes, usually for good things (an A on the test, a salary bonus). Wishes are magic thinking: incantations in the face of the unknown. They stem from the desire to manage the unknown future into tangible outcomes. In the case of the fear of failure, the wish is negative. Fearing failure boils down to wishing for a negative possibility of how things might work out—if only for the sake of closure and resolution.

Recognize that whatever you wish for, good or bad, the future remains unknown. Failure is a possibility, but not the only one. By "wishing" for failure you're unduly investing in just one of several possible outcomes, if only because it seems tangible. It's true: you can guarantee failure if you organize yourself to fail. The question is obvious: why put your energy there? Wishing may not get you anywhere, but you might as well wish for something good if you're going to wish at all.

▶▶10. EXCUSES ARE FEARS BY ANY OTHER NAME.

Still fearing the fear? The instant Freudian analysis didn't work for you? Here's some more help with fighting the most popular excuses for not acting on your desire to make films:

You're really good at what you're doing now.

Talent shouldn't be a punishment or a sentence. In addition to the job you currently hold, you might be really good at alpha-numeric filing, organizing children's birthday parties, or changing the starter in your car. Which doesn't mean you're doomed to doing these for the better part of your waking hours . . . or indeed, the best part of your life.

You're making a comfortable living.

There's no reason you can't go back to making it if you don't like filmmaking. Making a film or going to film school is not a life-time commitment, or a step that dooms you to take a vow of poverty. It's just something you want to try, one day or one semes-ter (thirteen weeks) at a time.

You might not be able to make a living at film.

Right now, without skills, you may not be able to make a liv-ing in film. But that's what training is for. Ever see the credits after a big Hollywood movie? The ones that go on and on . . . and on?

All of those people got paid. You may not get called to direct a feature right after school, but you will be able to get a job. Maybe not your dream job, but someplace to start. Filmmaking and entertainment are a $22 billion industry in L.A. alone. You won't have to wait for someone to die in order to get a job.

Besides, the skills you get from filmmaking won't only apply to film. They will let you contribute to any number of the traditional and emerging media—including television, theater, events planning, multimedia, and Web production. The master skill filmmaking teaches you—project management, or coordinating a multidimensional task so it gets completed on time and on budget—is something valued by employers in every field.

Your parents think it's a bad idea.

There are any number of answers to this one, including:

- Your parents didn't want you to move out.
- If they're always right, why did they dress you like that for your-third grade picture?
- Maybe you're actually looking for a chance to prove them wrong.
- They didn't like your girl or boyfriends, either. (Even if they were right, sometimes.)

You don't know how the industry will look in the future.

As the venues (and audiences) for mass media multiply all over the world, American media is the only one to carry a brand name for which audiences are willing to pay a premium. Mass media is one of America's most important exports, and our global market share is only expected to increase. We might answer this one differently if we were writing this book in France or the Sudan, but we're not.

Your sister is the creative one.

There's no such thing as a quota on the "creative ones" in any family.

You're afraid you're not creative enough.

Creativity is just another word for problem solving. One of the joys of filmmaking is that no matter who you are, you'll find some variety of problem you're particularly good at solving. If they're visual problems, then maybe you'll find yourself working as a cinematographer or production designer. If they're organizational problems, producing will fit. A knack for solving logic problems puts you in good stead to be an editor.

You're secretly afraid you're not cool enough.

The industry's social scene does work remarkably like high school's. At first the self-proclaimed "popular" kids seem to have a power no one can touch. But the same fate that befell your high school nemesis plays out here. In the end, the only thing that matters is the work. Only the work. Steady turtles win this race. You have a head start if you understand that hype doesn't play on the big screen, but good stories do.

Going to school will cost a lot.

Remember what your savvy friend said about the fashion disaster you picked up at a "bargain" price. It's not a bargain if you won't ever wear it. Relative to your chances of ever using it (i.e., zero), it's a complete and total waste of $9.99.

This wisdom works in reverse, too. You're not spending too much if you are getting what you want, and enough of it. You should think of film school as a studio, offering your film an array of services, equipment, and free crew. We urge you to do a cost-benefit analysis of your options, and only choose a school, or school at all, if it's the most efficient, technically practical, and financially sound means to make your film.

It's too late to start.

If you're strong enough to pick up a camera, you're young enough to be a filmmaker. There *is* a bias in the film industry in favor of youth, but don't make yourself its victim before anyone else tries to.

You're too young to start.

If you are old enough to master the directions to set up a Sony PlayStation then you're old enough. You don't have to wait to grow up to become the industry's average middle-aged white guy with an extra ten pounds in order to tell the world what you want it to know.

You don't know which part of filmmaking you like best.

The scientific method really does work here: trial and error, with error pointing you toward the crew jobs you might be better suited for. Film school forces you to do the jobs you didn't think you had any interest in, and that's a good thing. The competitive market for paying P.A. jobs will make you start in a department's outfield, but you'll still have a great view of the game, and a good sense of what job you want to pitch yourself for next.

If you're willing to work for free, you'll take a faster track to the thick of things. It's amazing what people will let you do if you'll do it for free, and show up every day. Ads in the classified section of the trades are full of people looking for people to do things for free—directing included.

You've heard that it's hard.

Isn't a challenge what you're after?

It's competitive.

No matter what industry you are in, you'll eventually recognize that the only person you're ever competing with is you. Give up now, and you've already given up on yourself.

You don't know anyone in Hollywood.

The people you learn how to make films with will grow up to be "the people in Hollywood." Meet them while you still have a chance at forging real friendships, through the shared experience of stalling the traffic, the landlords, or the cops, and you'll have no problem calling them later.

You're not ruthless enough.

In order to get your film made, you'll either discover this side of yourself, or how to attach yourself to someone who has enough of it to spare. It's a valuable quality to have access to when you need it.

You like watching films, but how do you know you'll like making them?

You won't know until you've tried. But then, we've never met anyone who didn't love seeing their first roll of film come back from the lab.

▸▸11. MAYBE YOU JUST WANT TO BE A ROCK STAR.

Deciding to be a filmmaker is deciding to live what for many people is a fantasy. You might as well choose the right one.

Your fantasy of being a filmmaker, for example, may have more to do with the freedom and intoxicating restlessness attributed to rock stars than it does with the reality of sitting in an editing room, alone, for hours.

So why not just do *that*? Pierce your tongue and get it over with! As a filmmaker, you do not get to have throngs of people paying to watch you sweat, you do not acquire groupies who will volunteer to do any number of things to your body, and you do not get the automatic justification to choose leather over "business casual" for your studio meetings.

You have, as far as we know, only this one life to live. Give yourself to anything you'd like to look back on when you're ninety-two. You won't ever get more than what you ask for, so set your sights both high and in the right place. Why bother struggling to be a filmmaker if you really want to be an archeologist, astronaut, or spy? Live your itinerary of desire, not someone else's.

Know you want to do something, but not quite sure what? Answer this: Which magazines do you pick up when you have a choice of any of them, and which do you actually read? *Variety* or *Vogue*? *Hollywood Reporter* or *Spin*? *American Cinematographer* or *BusinessWeek*? Or maybe it's really *Wired* that turns you on. Or *Martha Stewart's Living* that makes your palms sweat.

Every business stems from an obsession, and each requires you to be as or more obsessed than your coworkers in order to survive the long haul. Which magazines fill you with a sense of urgency and jealousy? Which do you need to read every word of? This is the field for which you feel the most authentic attraction. Believe us, your response is not universal. The dramas you find compelling— whether it's who bought what, who signed what, who shot what, or who wore what—are ridiculously irrelevant to other people.

Don't sublimate your real professional expectations and desires into a job that's not exactly "it"—even if that job is filmmaking. If you try to do what you really want and somehow fail, so what? Failure isn't an object sitting behind curtain number two. It takes a while to truly establish failure, as it does to truly experience success. When you're drawn to do something by love, success really doesn't have much to do with it. Success *is* doing the thing you love. Instead of anything else. So are you sure you don't want to be a rock star?

▸▸12. MAYBE YOU WANT TO BE DONALD TRUMP.

Money, fame, and power have little to do with the reality of most working filmmakers' lives and even less with the act of making films. Filmmaking is too demanding to be a means to an end. It's an end in itself.

Wait a minute, you say. Money, fame, and power are important to me. I don't want to make films in my basement that I show to myself in my basement, while I eat a TV dinner and get ready for my next shift at the poultry plant. I want a home in the Hollywood Hills, a blond date, a personalized parking space on the studio lot, a standing table for lunch, and at least one assistant to, you know, help me cope with the day-to-day burdens of being so fabulous.

If your most honest definition of success is the one they advertise on TV (lots of money), then maybe you should go to law school (or stay if you're already there), or get an MBA in information systems management. There are much, much more direct ways to make money than through film. You can make more money as a registered nurse than most crew people make, even when they're working steadily. And you'll get health benefits.

▶▶ 13. OR MAYBE YOU WANT TO BE MICHAEL EISNER.

Just as we have sneaking suspicions that under every executive is a frustrated filmmaker, we have equal suspicions that many struggling filmmakers would be happier in plush office surroundings. There is no moral hierarchy to jobs in the film business. The only "wrong" is lying to yourself.

The concept of a salary, for example, might have its appeal, as might being the one who gets to say "red light, green light." Or, you may find out that you just hate production. We wouldn't blame you.

Beware, though. Because an industry career is not necessarily any more secure in the long run than being a (successful) filmmaker—the regular paycheck, expense account, and everything with it can disappear overnight if you get fired. When shake-ups happen at the top of studio rosters, as they do regularly, the aftershocks are felt throughout the organization. When your langoustine lunching buddy who gave you your job leaves or is kicked out, you may be next. Suddenly the projects you were working on no longer fit the new "direction" the organization is moving in. And neither do you.

▶▶ 14. MAYBE YOU JUST WANT TO LIVE ON A CUL-DE-SAC.

Ozzie and Harriet were not freelance grips. It's not easy to maintain a stable lifestyle on a freelancer's cash flow. The freelance path may not be for you if, like most people:

- You like a regular paycheck
- You want health insurance

- You would like a 401(k) (i.e., retirement savings)
- You like a regular place to go to every day
- You like regular hours
- You don't like spending more of your time looking for jobs than doing them

We need to stress, wanting any or all of this stuff is normal. This is how most of America runs: with people working at regular jobs, with regular hours, and managing families, junior soccer leagues, and retirement plans.

Try, as an exercise, to add up your current monthly expenses. Divide by a five-day workweek and figure out what you would need to make at a day job to cover your expenses. Use the same total of monthly expenses and see how much you would need to charge a film production per day for your services if you worked an optimistic ten days a month. Does this seem feasible? If not, you may have to do some lifestyle restructuring, debt reduction, and the like before you can comfortably swing with the free-lancers.

Working in film has real costs, too. There is a certain amount of overhead associated with being a successful freelance professional. David Davidson, a friend who supports himself and his independent filmmaking as a freelance art director, has found that it costs him $20,000 per year to maintain an extensive kit of tools and supplies, and slew of phone, fax, cell, and pager numbers that he needs to stay in the business. This includes having a large, insured SUV kept in top running order so that he can drive out to the desert on a moment's notice carrying five suckling pigs or a pile of down pillows for the shoot he has just been hired on. Trying to build a career in L.A. as a freelancer with an impractical car, say, a 1973 Fiat convertible that continuously breaks down, is not charming—it's stupid.

To successfully freelance, you must be similarly ready, willing, and able to work 24/7. This has its costs, including opportunity cost. Opportunity cost is the total value of what you give up when you choose to do something else. In the case of freelance work versus a normal job, it includes, among other things, money, a pension plan, and a position that society can acknowledge. Invest ten years in anything and you can start to enjoy real progress. Ten years out of college, your investment banking friends will be on to buying their second homes. Your law school friends will have paid off their student loans. Your nest-oriented friends will have their second or third child. Your academic friends will have Ph.D. after their names. You'll have, maybe, a few finished screenplays and, maybe, your first sale.

Despite all their houses and degrees, after ten years of the same job and the stress of working on someone else's behalf, your friends may actually be jealous of you. Still, before you go further, you need to ask yourself: after ten years, will you be jealous of yourself? Or of them?

▶▶ 15. MAYBE YOU DON'T KNOW WHO YOU WANT TO BE.

Making films is an expensive way to find yourself, if that's what you're really after.

FINDING YOURSELF: A COST COMPARISON.

Spiritual retreat in Santa Fe
Deva Foundation's 4-session course: $800

Trekking in Nepal
Peter Owens' Asian Treks' 36-day trek in Nepal ($1,600)
Plus round-trip airfare from L.A. ($1,700): $3,300

Freudian analysis
Three years, five times a week ($100/session): $78,000

Film school

Three years' tuition ($48,000) plus three years' living expenses ($42,000)

Plus film production costs ($20,000): $110,000

Financing your own feature

The credit card version: anywhere from $500 upward depending on how many new cards they let you sign up for, $500 to infinity, or beyond

3

IF ALL YOU REALLY WANT TO DO IS DIRECT, WHAT ARE YOU WAITING FOR?

▶▶16. THE MAGIC WORDS.

You don't need permission. No one asks you for your security clearance. It takes something a little more subtle. To be a director, you have to be able to say, "I care."

You must be willing to take a strong and tenacious point of view with regard to the story you are telling. You have to be willing to say why this story is meaningful to you, and what your personal relationship is to it. This puts you in a vulnerable place, which is why, when faced with it, most people don't actually enjoy directing.

Remember when you raised your hand in the third grade for liking a book, movie, or song, and the other kids laughed at you? You were uncool for liking something. For caring. At thirteen, "I don't care" and "I don't know" became key phrases. You still use them when you're nervous.

The reason it's hard to direct a film is that you have to say, "I care" a lot. Not just "I want to make this film," which is like saying, "I care." But also "I want the camera here" (not here) or "I want this color paint for the walls" (not that one). That's "I care." Directing a film means taking the path of most resistance.

Every time you express your care or concern, you take a risk. For starters, there's the risk that other people won't see the point and will, basically, laugh at you. Then there's the risk of sharing your secrets; when you bring them out into the open, they can't be secret anymore. Neither can your soul. Saying that you care involves revealing your ideas of what you think is beautiful, moving, and meaningful. Your heart will be on your sleeve. Cast and crew will have their own opinions about what you're sharing, and they'll share them. They'll challenge you to change how you feel about your own thoughts and feelings. Are you ready?

One tack directors take to avoid all of this stuff is to pin the "care" on somebody else. At film school pitches, would-be directors talk about how *other* people will care. "It's an important subject," or "This film can make a difference to a lot of [other] people," they say. The logic being employed here, unfortunately, is that it is more important to prove that others care than it is to prove that you do.

Another version of not having to say "I care" is to make a film like other people have made. In Hollywood this protective (conservative) instinct has given rise to the genre, the subgenre, and the sequel. In TV it's why there are so many "judges" and *Friends*. At film school it's why there are so many films featuring: young boys losing their fathers, young boys finding their fathers, homeless people finding lost children, small children finding lost pets, and young men finding themselves.

There's nothing intrinsically wrong with these themes, just as long as the director cares enough about them to make them particular (i.e., personal), and therefore original. As painfully dull as the genre-fied versions of these stories tend to be in successive screenings, making them tends to be painful, period. Set by set, prop by prop, take by take, it's exhausting to do so much work for something you don't particularly believe in.

When a director can't find a way to believe in the material, the audience can smell the cynical calculations on the screen. Asking people to spend time watching or making your film is either a crazy or a noble thing. It depends. On how much you're ready to care.

▶▶17. WHY YOU HAVE TO BE MORE VULNERABLE THAN THE NEXT GUY.

The audience walks into a theater, sits down, and, as the lights go down, opens up its wounds. They have not come to experience your pain. They have come to relive their own experience, in the quiet hope of either recovering its sensations or relieving themselves of its burdens.

Your film is nothing more or less than a conduit for an audience's own emotional experience. Your protagonist serves as the face on which an audience projects and recovers its own feelings and its own vulnerabilities to the slings and arrows that assail the human spirit.

Your film succeeds by providing an audience with an opportunity for empathy. Empathy is the film's emotional Swiss army knife: the gatekeeper to an audience's feelings.

For the transference to work, the protagonist must be endowed with a rich, compelling, and sympathetic heart and mind that the audience can believe in as its "own." Creating such characters depends on your powers of empathy—your capacity to feel another's emotions as your own. Empathy is what is meant by putting the "personal" into your filmmaking. Your feelings for another character or another person are, of course, derived from your own experience. The most honest way to know what your characters feel is to know yourself.

Not that you must create autobiography, but you should endow your work with an emotional logic derived from real experience. Empathy with your own feelings lets you experience empathy for your characters and from this information create emotionally accurate portrayals. When characters' emotions are real, the audience in turn can experience empathy.

You must be willing to accept that the process of filmmaking is the prospect of putting your own naked desire on a wide screen. We are not referring to sexual desire per se, although that is a huge part of it, but the desire to connect in its largest sense.

You must be just as open as your eventual audience, if not more so, because you must take the lead. If your protagonist does not struggle under sufficient burdens, the audience will lose respect for him, thinking, "Those problems are not nearly as bad as mine," followed by, "Why should I care about this character at all?"

If you're worried about being too exposed, remember that the audience does not usually know you and, in any case, does not usually care who you are. It's their pain they care about and theirs they feel in that dark room. Let them have it.

▸▸18. TAKE CREATIVE RESPONSIBILITY. NO ONE ELSE WILL.

At our film schools, films are made in a competitive fishbowl environment where everyone can see what the other team is doing. The disconcerting gaze of a gaggle of students and teachers is enough to make anyone nervous. Especially since there's a group tendency to rank winners and losers. A "popular film" emerges, and from there the games are similar to high school's—with some people desperate to hang out with the "winner" team while distancing themselves from their own "loser" crew and film.

No one ever knows how well a film is going to work until it screens in front of an audience. But when the feeling, or even just the perception, of audience disdain starts, it can easily sweep along the crew. Eager to act like they have nothing to do with even a potential failure, they check out of defending or even associating themselves with the film. Personal responsibility turns to cheap blame, with the director becoming the fall guy for the film and everything that was un-fun and un-cool about the shoot or the film.

When we were at school, teachers actually (if inadvertently) encouraged this response. Crew members met in classes according to their discipline (editing, cinematography, producing, etc.), which frequently devolved to complaint sessions about the director's mistakes. As in: "The film just doesn't edit together and it's the director's fault." And "I know the shot's dark, but it's the director's fault." Instead of encouraging crew to assert their opinions and fix their own messes, we had teachers who nodded along to the unfairness of it all.

We make a point of having weekly meetings during preproduction, where everyone can share their ideas, both for their department's work and the film in general. On one film, these meetings were less fun than a tax return. Sensing the possibility of failure, no one wanted to contribute anything that could be traced back to them.

Such group dynamics play on and reinforce a victim mentality that does nothing for anyone. Victims are fundamentally reviled because—by their own assertion—they have no power, except through complaint and manipulated sympathy. Don't be a victim. When you commit to a project, do so for better and worse. Do the same on other people's films. From the moment you agree to work on a film, you share in its failure as well as its success. So put your attention into making the best, instead of the worst, of the situation.

▶▶19. ORIGINALITY IS ALL THE AUTHORITY YOU NEED.

Everyone fears the impostor. Actually, everyone fears being the impostor. Here's how it goes: "What gives me the right to write when this is the language of Shakespeare (or Billy Wilder, or Joan Didion . . . or whoever it is that scares you)?" Or, "What gives me the right to make films when films are the creations of Antonioni, Fellini, and Malick?"

To this grand and sweeping fear we have one sweeping answer: because no one has ever tried to create as you.

Your work may not be "better" than that of others before you, but it can be unique. Originality is a virtue. No one has written a story about your grandmother's birthday. No one has thought or felt what you did as you were going to sleep last night. No one has made a film of exactly what it felt like when you fell in love for the first time. No one will, unless you do.

The question of "voice," along with that of "vision," is clouded with unnecessary smoke and mirrors. Both are just other names for something everyone has by birthright: an original perspective. The genetic package you were born with is yours alone. Add the variables and textures brought by your life experiences, and you have both a voice and a vision unlike anyone else's.

The things you notice, as well as the things you take for granted, are the result of your unique perspective. When you point a camera at a scene, what you leave out is as important as what you put in . . . and is inevitably different than the choices someone else would make.

Don't worry about authority. If you need to say something, it needs to be said. Has it been said before? Probably. But not in the specific way in which you understand it and need to say it. "Love is blind," "All that glitters isn't gold," "History repeats itself"—all of these things have been said. But maybe not by you, and not to the people you need to reach.

You might not know offhand what your voice sounds like or what it wants to say. That's what creating is for. You'll find out what you know, and how you sound, not by guessing, but by doing. You'll sound strange at first. You may not think you sound like yourself. Keep going. Your inner voice will start to sound like your creative voice, and your creative voice will start sounding like you.

No one can ever be as good at being you as you are, naturally. You aren't an impostor when you play yourself. Creating original characters is hard. Which makes the fact that you are totally different than anyone who ever lived rather astonishing. Take advantage of it.

▸▸ 20. PAY ATTENTION, EVEN WHEN ORDERING ICE CREAM.

Being a good director means paying attention to what people say, what they want, what they need, and how they get it. You have to be able to read wants and needs conveyed by an actor in a performance so that you can reconcile these with what you have in mind for the character. This is a skill to develop through practice, on and off the set.

Pay attention to the unconscious messages people give when they're asking for something. Notice the differences. In line at the ice cream store, everyone has different ways of asking for what's supposed to be the same thing. What with the subconscious, we're rarely asking for what we think we're asking for.

In addition to the ice cream, some are asking to feel guilty, some to have their guilt absolved. A father's trying to get a child to laugh; another's trying to get his kid to shut up. A boy is more interested in that girl behind the counter than the difference between rocky road and mocha almond fudge. In other words, most real-life situations are loaded with subtext. If you want your films to seem real, they should be too.

If you're drawn to filmmaking, you may have already had significant practice as an observer—of yourself as well as others. There's someone in most families who takes the job of smoothing over arguments, helping everyone understand what everyone else is feeling. That might be you. You might be someone who writes down things or laughs when no one knows why. Films are made by observers who carry a camera in their mind's eye and look through it from a place of empathy and curiosity.

▸▸21. DIRECTING IS A GOOD EXCUSE FOR SPYING.

Directors need to sharpen the same skills that private investigators do: the capacity to notice definitive clues—the specific details that reveal and inform characters, and on which a plot can twist. Narrowing in on these details in your scripts' descriptions helps keep them short and effective. Leveraging them in your filmmaking is a way to develop a powerful visual shorthand.

For more practice in the art of observation, we recommend

reading mysteries by Patricia Cornwell and Agatha Christie, wherein the plot resolution most often turns on the smallest of details. Exercise your private-eye by:

- Sitting alone at restaurants and taking notes. Without hearing people's words, try to understand what their actions say based on their actions.
- Sitting in on court cases and looking for signs that indicate when people are lying.
- Flipping through TV stations with the sound off, gauging your first impressions of on-camera talents' attitudes, and noticing when they don't necessarily mesh with what's been scripted.
- Analyzing cars—interior and exterior—for what they reveal about the owners.
- Looking at the way someone's dressed to identify the one thing that if taken away would significantly alter their projected identity.
- Watching couples and families in public places to notice what their gestures reveal about their relationships, including how power and dominance is established or maintained.

Don't leave yourself out of your spying. The more you're able to clearly gauge your own habits, behaviors, and assumptions, the more sensitive you'll be in understanding those of others.

4

NAPKINS, STOPLIGHTS, AND SHOWERS

▶▶ 22. WHY WRITING IS MORE IMPORTANT THAN TAKING YOUR VITAMINS.

Learn to write scripts that sell and you'll literally be able to write your own ticket to a commercially successful filmmaking career. We can't make this point too strongly: if you have any desire to direct or to have any real control over your career in film or television, invest your blood, sweat, and tears in learning to write.

A director without a script is just a director. A producer without a script is no one. A writer without a terrific, full-length feature script is wasting everyone's time.

Write a commercially viable script and you've created the very opportunity for a film where there wasn't one before. Scripts are this industry's equivalent of business plans: the starting point for other people's investment. Explicitly, the script narrates the film's story. Implicitly, it suggests both a potential audience and, by extension, potential profits. Scripts that sell do so by convincing investors that the realized film will deliver a significant portion of a financially significant audience.

Selling a script is not selling a piece of art but rather a ticket to profits. If they smell the money, you won't have to bother convincing them that it's art, or that you're an artist. You can take the money and make your own film or, with enough leverage or chutzpah, negotiate to stay attached as the director.

Of course, you can write scripts that you plan to produce yourself, and never worry about getting money back for your time or expenses if you can afford it. In which case, you can skip the parts in the next two chapters that relate to writing "professionally" (i.e., for other people's money).

Consider this, though: John Sayles, the very apostle of independent filmmaking, has produced and directed a lifetime of uncompromised films aided by the money he picks up as an (often uncredited) script doctor on studio films. There are lots of ways to use the writing skills you develop, and lots of ways to use the money.

▶▶ 23. YOUR SHORT FILM IS ONLY AS GOOD AS YOUR FEATURE SCRIPT.

A year, two, three, or more gone. Countless nights of sleep lost. Your credit card limits reached. Your relationships peaked. Massive piles of laundry reek. Finally, the screening. Producers, managers, and agents will be there, promising—at least, in the fantasies that have kept you going all this time—some kind of happy ending.

What will you say when they call the next day with just one question: "So, do you have a script?"

If your answer is no, it will all have been for nothing. Really. Don't believe us, and you're setting yourself up for the same trap that generations of haggard film school graduates want to warn you about.

"Jack" (not his real name) worked very hard as a director in his first year at film school making warm-hearted films with strong narrative appeal. He worked very hard his second year, too, directing a longer, warm-hearted film with strong narrative appeal.

His film, more than any other student work in the school's recent memory, received an extraordinary response. Agents, managers, and producers deluged him with praise and invitations. Studios hurried to arrange private screenings of his film for their executives. A major cable network gave him an award, broadcast his film, and flew him out to New York for a gala event, escorting him with limousines and surrounding him with recording stars. The

Directors Guild of America gave him a directing award and an executive from Robert Redford's production company approached him with the sincere desire to work with him on his next project.

"Do you have a script?" she asked.

He didn't. Not finished, anyway. He gave the right answer, under the circumstances: "I've got something I've been working on, but it's not there yet."

"When will it be done?" she asked.

"Six weeks," he answered.

The company called before the six weeks were up, at the six weeks, and after the six weeks. Each time reiterating the desire to work with him. Each time reasserting the desire to see his script.

He panicked.

Six more weeks passed.

He shut down.

He couldn't finish it. In some ways, he was further from being done than when he had started. He finally had to call and confess that he didn't know when he would finish the script.

It's been a year. No one's called in a while. He has a completed script now, but in some ways he's back where he started. Along with too many other beginning filmmakers who took this very expensive road back to square one.

Among them "Cameron," who flagellates herself for having made the mistake not once but twice. The first time: after her short student film screened for agents and producers. She accepted invitations to lunch, guilelessly expecting they would come with offers for some variation on a three-picture deal. It took a while for her to understand what producers meant by the question "So, what are you working on next?" She had thought *they* were supposed to tell her what they wanted her to do next. After a short while the interest, calls, and newly befriended agent faded away. Flash forward. Cameron's second student film won a major award from a prestigious international film festival. Producers and agents called again. This time she had a script. Indeed, she had two. But neither of them were truly finished (i.e., saleable and producible). More meetings and free lunches ensued. But again, after the espresso, she went home with nothing to take to the bank.

When we spoke to Cameron, she was on the verge of committing the mistake for the third time. This time, with a feature she and her husband put all their money and last year into. Although it's done, has already screened in its first festival, and got a great review in one of the trades, neither Cameron nor her husband have a saleable script ready. What do you think will happen next?

Because beginning filmmakers spend so much of themselves making short films, most fall under a hypnotized delusion that the short film itself will get them the happy ending. It's hard for them to believe that all that work and money adds up, at best, to the invitation to submit a script to someone's office. As if working day and night on your film hadn't been enough.

It wasn't. Your short film isn't enough, because there is a limited commercial market for short films and agents and producers can't make any real money from them. Your short is, at best, a prompt for them to ask to see more of your work—the kind they can make money on.

They want a script. That's all they want, all they ever wanted, and all they will ever want. Whether from you or someone else. Seeing your film gave them the idea that it might come from you. If you don't have one, they'll look somewhere else. And you'll have blown it.

Why can't they just take you as the director for something they already have? Because they already have directors, more than they can use. Directing is something that just about everyone thinks they can do. Favors are already promised. Their receptionist wants to direct. Directors are not scarce. What's scarce is material that can make them money. No one can ever have enough of that. Your demonstration of directing talent is just the long way of convincing them that you might have something they want to read.

You've spent $64,000 and more years than you want to count just so you can get an invitation into someone's office. Better have a great script so that they'll invite you back.

▶▶ 24. ALWAYS BE WRITING.

How many people do you know who work hard, consistently, at one thing?

Film attracts dilettantes. If you are not one, you will stand out like a Fabergé egg in a supermarket carton of ordinary ones. When they open you, they will find wonderful material with structure and intrinsic value, not runny, undifferentiated yolks. We're not sure how far we can go with this analogy, but we think you know what we're getting at.

Our friend Lisa's mother says, "Geniuses finish things." You could read this a couple of ways. One reading is that it takes genius to finish something. The way we'd like to read it, however, is that no one would know about a genius's work if he or she hadn't finished it.

Think about how ridiculously good you've gotten at your day job. All as a result of showing up. In the studio days, writers were workers, like everyone else. They showed up for daily shifts and wrote. Every day. No la-di-da artist's excuses.

The bad habits society assigns to, and accepts from, artists are just a sign of its disdain. You wouldn't let your doctor get away with showing up late, or saying that she just didn't feel like treating you today. Society respects doctors, and the high standards for doctors are a sign of this respect.

If you don't treat your writing, or other creative work, with a similar degree of serious respect, you're buying into the mythology of artists as flaky, marginal, and ultimately disposable members of society. If you don't practice, it's testimony to the fact that writing doesn't get society's respect, and it doesn't have yours.

▶▶ 25. TWENTY MINUTES OF WRITING EVERY DAY IS BETTER THAN WAITING FOR INSPIRATION ANY DAY.

Make the decision to write first thing every morning, and you won't have to agonize over it every day.

Make the decision now, and from now on you need only get up, shower maybe, and hit it. Rather than spending the same time wondering whether you should write today (of course), whether you feel like it (no, but that has nothing to do with it), and whether there's something you wouldn't rather be doing instead (of course, but so what?).

If your parents hadn't made you brush your teeth twice a day, would you do it now? They made it easy by reducing it to habit and removing it from debate. Sit around thinking about brushing your teeth and you've wasted more time than it would have taken to do it. The idea is to reduce writing to a habit rather than treat it like an operatic performance. Remove it from the list of decisions you have to think about and agonize over.

Start, and it's over, nearly as quickly. Like a shot. Add up those twenty minutes and at the end of a week you've written for two hours. This is your version of those dauntingly righteous graphs that show that if you had only put two dollars in the bank when you were eight years old you could retire now. You don't need to invest a lot, but you do want to invest early. Because everything you put in compounds like interest. Write something down once and you don't ever have to again. From now on, you can just add to it.

Anything but writing is procrastination. With obvious exceptions for taking care of kids or going to the hospital. But only if it's really an emergency. Breakfast, sex, and the trip to the dry cleaners can all happen after that crucial twenty minutes. The time it took to read this section could have been spent writing.

▸▸26. TIME IS MADE, NOT FOUND.

This is for the people who gave the inevitable "I don't have time" response to the last section. If you don't have time, how did you read the newspaper this morning? Or surf with your remote last night?

You don't have time to write, you *make* time.

The real limiting factor is not time but energy. If you don't have energy, it's partly because you're wasting it in this kind of argument with us, and yourself. But also because you're not unleashing the energy you actually get from writing. It's like exercise. At first it takes energy, then it gives back as much and more.

You can make time by cutting the waste out of wasted time. Predict and redirect the dull lag times that inevitably find their way into every day, and turn them into productive use.

Places to find—that is, *make*—time where you may not have looked already include wherever you can bring a notebook: the laundry room, the drive-through line at McDonald's, the traffic on the 405 freeway, the block you walk your dog around, the movie theater seat before the previews start, the commuter train, and the not-so-express supermarket line. Then there's also: at the office before work starts (plan on getting to work twenty minutes early: the traffic will be that much lighter, so you might score twenty-five minutes); at the office, even after work starts (keep a file open on your computer and sneak visits to it); during a drive, with a friend, talk out stories on your way to and from the birthday party, fishing trip, work, or wherever; wherever you're not too embarrassed to talk into a tape recorder (not for anyone else to transcribe, but as a way to focus your thoughts and to keep your ideas moving); while reading or watching a movie (keep your reading and video watching in tune with the subject and themes of what you're writing, and take notes about your own film while you do either).

Everyone spends some of their time inefficiently. That's the time you need to make use of.

▸▸ 27. A ROOM OF YOUR OWN.

A friend said he discovered he had a muse as soon as he gave her a regular address where she could find him. Pick a chair, any chair, and sit there at the same time every day. Your own muse will eventually find you.

If that chair's in your apartment, you're lucky. You don't need to go far. You don't even need to shower.

If your room doesn't work for you, it doesn't. If you like the rumble and sighing and page turning of other people for company, you're not alone. Find a place where people go to be alone, together. Not a place where people hold breakfast meetings, with loud or otherwise distracting conversations. Your alone-ness should be the norm. Look for a place with tables for one person. And refill coffee.

Test the waters. If it doesn't feel right, it isn't. Leave. If it does, stay. Stay past the point of traditional welcome and see what happens. If no one notices, or if, indeed, the place welcomes you and what you're doing, you're home.

If you live in New York, try the Hungarian Pastry Shop on 114th and Amsterdam. In L.A., try Santa Monica's Novel Café or Silverlake's The Coffee Table. These places are homes to a nest of writers, and they are subtly but firmly self-policed by useful codes:

- Don't interrupt someone's work (or even apparent procrastination) unless invited to.
- If a fellow writer is being unwillingly interrupted, come to her aid.
- Take messages for each other.
- Watch each other's stuff.
- Limit the cell phone use. If you must use one, do so outside.
- Never ask, "Are you done yet?" but celebrate the times when someone is.

The last rule is: don't start a romance with a regular there, because when it breaks up, you'll have to fight for custody of the place. This is Camille's rule from regretted experience. After bitter words she and the ex finally settled on assigned time shifts at the café.

Everyone needs a room of their own. Your most important support relationship might not be with a person but with a place you go to every day.

▸▸28. DON'T READ WHAT YOU WRITE
(UNTIL AFTER YOU'VE WRITTEN IT).

Einstein said we couldn't simultaneously prepare for and prevent war. Likewise, you can't simultaneously create and criticize your own work.

What they teach you from kindergarten on is how to be critical. How to correct your own mistakes and those of others. From "What's wrong with this picture?" through "What's wrong with this essay?" Critical powers are quite different skills than impulsive creative ones. Not that criticism doesn't involve creativity. But the act, like the cart, should come after the horse.

There are literally an infinite number of ways to write any story, any sentence, any phrase. Writing is largely a process of elimination. But you won't know what to eliminate, and what to keep, until you see the whole picture. You won't know the whole picture until you write it.

Writing is a process of revelation and self-education. As you write, you learn what you know, and see more clearly what you don't know. You write your way to writing.

Don't stop yourself from having a thought before you have a chance to explore where it is taking you. Don't assume it doesn't fit or is irrelevant to what you're writing or doing, or is getting off the track you think you are supposed to be on.

You might not know what your project is about until you allow your unconscious to explore what the real meaning and scope of your idea actually is. If you keep censoring your creativity, you will get nowhere. Or you will get somewhere, but it might be a much more obvious somewhere than if you had given yourself more creative freedom.

Starving yourself of writing opportunities feeds your self-censor. Immersion and repetition in the act of writing will allow you to move slowly through surface preoccupations to points of deeper meaning in your writing. The subconscious doesn't operate well under a spotlight. It likes a little dim, low-lit space to tool around in. Let it. What's the worst that can happen? That you find out what you're really thinking?

▶▶29. WRITER'S BLOCK K.O.

Writer's block is the uneasy mix of your editor's and writer's voices fighting each other like bickering siblings in the back of the car. Pull over, slap them, and teach them to take turns.

We were about to erase the last two lines but took our own advice.

If you can't get rid of the editing voice through negotiation, you'll have to fake it out. Here are some tricks:

- Write for a specified period of time. Sit down at your kitchen counter and put a little pizza in the broiler to cook. Write like a madman for the fifteen minutes it takes for the pizza's cheese to bubble. Stop. Eat the pizza. Repeat until you complete your writing goal.
- Remove the goal. For once, try to remove the pressure of meeting a certain page or content goal for the day; give yourself permission to wander.
- Write your script in another language, by hand on construction paper with crayons, or in any way that frees you from the pressure of performance.
- Write what you want. Eliminate the dissonance between what you should be writing and what you want to write.
- Go somewhere different. Sit in your kitchen sink and write some pages there if that is the last unexplored, underexploited writing setting in your life.
- Add jeopardy. Take whatever situation that's stumping or boring you and add the most absurd or extreme element of jeopardy you can for that moment, short of a boulder falling out of a clear blue sky. Jeopardy is what audiences watch for

and what will keep you engaged in the material as you work on it.

- Write what comes first, first. Write without stopping or correcting. Every time you stop to read, correct, or write over something, it's your critical voice taking over and causing you to lose momentum. You can always write another line, next. Just don't erase the first.

- Write an e-mail to a friend about what you're trying to write and about any problems you might be having. Include some notes about what you're really trying to say. Send the letter and get the response. You can write entire pieces this way. E-mail offers the chance to have conversations, through words. Which is what writing is.

- Use/make use of slash marks. As you're typing, if there's a different word/phrase/thought that comes to you, don't force yourself to choose one at that moment. It will cramp your progress/momentum. Just write them all out—as many possibilities as come to you/plague you. Then you already have material/you have set yourself up for a satisfying editing process. Just going through and making choices, when that's your dedicated task, will give you a constructive/safe way to guide your rewriting/your refinement of what you mean to say.

- Call a friend, tell your story, and tape it. If it doesn't flow out the first time, ask your friend if you can keep trying until it does. Have your friend tell the story back to you—you'll hear what sticks for them and what doesn't.

- Go away for the weekend by yourself; limit your phone calling and contact with the world. Do bring, or make sure you have access to, nutritious food and, if necessary, air conditioning. You don't want the very matter of basic survival to be a distraction. Take this retreat concept to an extreme if necessary. Have a friend drop you off (and promise to pick you up from) at a place with limited public transportation possibilities. Such isolation and even sensory deprivation is essentially what fancy writing colonies offer, by invitation only, with their amenity-poor cabins isolated from one another, rules against talking to anyone, and food available only through delivery of a basket outside your door.

- Go to a bookstore and notice which section draws your attention and interest. If this content is not currently involved in your writing, try including it. Think about why you're writing about something else.

- Take a (time-limited) reading break. Read something well written. Recognize that your writing will rarely be better than the quality of what you're reading.

- Write your material in something other than script format, preferably a format that you are not very familiar with—a country song, for example. This frees you up because it makes you realize that all writing involves some kind of form, and the kind you're attempting right now has its own learning curve. You may just be at a steep part of it.

- Recognize that two hours is a full day for many, if not most writers. That's the secret. Most don't write for more than two to three hours a day. But they do write during that time. One health trivia website claims that writing burns up nearly as many calories in a half hour as canoeing. Whatever the case may be, writing is exhausting physically, mentally, and emotionally. If you've achieved a cumulative two to three hours, you may have done what you can—if not for that whole day, at least for that sitting. Get up, do something else, and come back to it when it feels like a new day.

- Remember that you get to rewrite. Rewriting is in some ways easier, less existential. You've narrowed the infinite possibilities into the sentences on the page. But in order to have something to rewrite, you need to put something down. Think of writing your first draft merely as preparation for your real job, of rewriting.

- If you're coming up blank, it may be that you've exercised all the obvious examples. You've run out of the plots you already unconsciously know from watching TV, and the genre solutions to your story don't work. Now you have to dig inside yourself to find something worth writing about.

▸▸ 30. WRITE ON DAYS YOU DON'T WANT TO WRITE.

Your desire, or lack of desire, to write on any given day has nothing to do with how well you'll do. Granted, discouragement may keep you from sitting down, in which case you'll prove your own point: you can't write anything that day. If you make a point of sitting down even on the days you don't want to, however, you'll believe what we're saying. You may not want to do it, but you can do it. Just as well as on the so-called good days.

It's like exercising. Your body isn't less ready to work out on the days you don't want to. The muscles are just where you left them yesterday. Get on the Stairmaster and do what you can, one step at a time. You'll come to the end of your session one way or another. Nothing says, in fact, that it won't be the day of your best workout so far.

5

FIX THE SCRIPT, THE REST WILL FOLLOW

▶▶ 31. THREE-ACT STRUCTURE IS NOT THE ONLY WAY, BUT IT DOESN'T HURT IF YOU WANT A JOB.

The way you tell a story is as personal and specific as the story you tell. Translate your story to film and the same is true. The way you tell a filmed story, using the possibilities of image and sound, is entirely up to you.

This said, most every studio film made in the last twenty years follows the same storytelling convention, or structure. Three acts. A clear beginning (Act 1: 1–20 minutes), middle (Act 2: 40–60 minutes), and end (Act 3: 1–20 minutes). A singular protagonist (morally strong, but in other ways weak) and a tangible antagonist (morally weak, but in all other ways strong). An evident starting place (when something goes out of balance in the world of the protagonist) and end point (when the protagonist lets go of his or her desire to bring back the world as it was, and accepts the change that is). A noble journey for the protagonist (from seeking something he or she wants—such as money—to accepting something he or she truly needs—such as love), and therein the moral.

This is the "formula," and it has helped make American films the world's most popular. What's not broken no studio intends to fix. While executives may be shortsighted to ignore that there are potentially any number of other ways to tell a story (Shakespeare's have five acts, for example), you are wrong to believe that you can change their minds with one script. If you want to sell them a script for money, your best chances are to write one the way they like it.

Any number of books detail how to follow the laws of three-act structure. Some make the intellectually corrupt claim that there is something inherently aesthetically superior about this way. Nonsense. Commercial success is another story, though. Three-act structure is the worldwide financial winner by far. *Jaws, Star Wars*, and *Rocky*, among many, many others followed this pattern to the bank.

If you're interested in being a "commercial" (that is, paid) writer or director, you have an interest in learning about what sells to audiences and, by extension, to the producers who seek to sell to them.

Adam Collis made a wonderful short film, "Mad Boy, I'll Blow Your Blues Away. Be Mine." Emotionally lyrical, funny, heartfelt, and structurally clear. Adam had to clear his answering machine four times the day after the screening to keep up with the messages from producers, agents, and managers. All were eager to meet someone who could so clearly execute work with clear three-act structure and narrative closure. Adam signed with agents at William Morris and within months landed a deal to direct a $13 million film for Fox.

Unfortunately, we have to contrast the "Mad Boy" success story with that of another USC film, "The Paraclete," by Velko Milosevich and Brooks Rawlins. "The Paraclete" is the single best student film we've ever seen and could ever hope to see. It is a story about childhood, homeland, the impossible loss of both to violence, as well as the dreadful sweetness of memory, powerless to bring back either. It is simultaneously delicate and violent, direct and mysterious, convulsively felt, and absolutely original. The film's storytelling structure—as original and emotionally felt as the film is as a whole—has the eloquence of a sonnet. But it is not linear, or composed of three consecutive acts. It has not inspired the same confidence among producers of more traditionally structured work, or the agents and managers who sell to them. At least, not nearly on the scale that "Mad Boy" did. We find this absurd, since to us the film's achievements are proof enough that these guys could handle anything. But we're not the producers. Yet.

▶▶ 32. TAKE STORY MEETINGS WITH EIGHT-YEAR-OLDS.

Eight-year-olds really don't care if they hurt your feelings. They don't worry about whether you think they're stupid, or whether you'll ever work with them again. They love stories. With or without Harrison Ford in the lead. They won't fill in the blanks if it doesn't work for them. They'll just ask you what's going on. They won't tell you they like it and then tell everyone else they hate it. They're man enough to tell you it stinks. Or that it's BOOR-ing.

With eight-year-olds, as with your worst fear of a studio executive, it's easy to tell if they don't get something. They'll look at you with a blank expression and say, "I don't get it." You'll say, "Which part?" They'll say, "I just don't get *it*."

If they don't get it, chances are you don't really know your story well enough. If you understand something well, you can explain it at any level to anyone.

Tell a kid your story and see what happens. The first clue will come in the telling. You'll skip the boring parts and the parts that are only in there because you worked so hard on them. What you leave out of the telling is significant; it probably doesn't belong in your film. As in, if an eight-year-old can understand your story without it, why have it?

▶▶ 33. LOVE YOUR FRIENDS FOR CRITICIZING YOUR WORK—ESPECIALLY AT THE SCRIPT STAGE.

Don't shoot the messenger. You're asking them to give notes, meaning you already know there's trouble. Don't punish them for it.

You're angry at needing help, and asking for it. You're angry that they know you need help. Whatever anger and frustration you feel is anger and frustration at yourself, so get it under control. A fresh eye can help you exponentially as long as you pick your readers well.

Scripts are impossible to read for people who are unfamiliar with the format. It's difficult for them to visualize what you're indicating on the page, or to fill in the spots that are supposed to be left unsaid. Scripts, unlike novels, are only blueprints for the final product—not detailed illustrations. Pick someone who knows about what you're supposed to leave in and leave out.

If you don't have a friend who fits this bill, there are companies and individuals who can be hired to give you a professional opinion. Look for their ads at the back of the trades and entertainment-themed magazines. Rates start around fifty dollars and the name-brand guys charge upward of five hundred dollars. Don't expect more than what you're paying them for—an opinion, not a solution.

When you get professional readers' notes back, they will probably be in the language of development, a *lingua franca* derived from the weekends executives (and aspiring executives) have spent in Robert McKee's and Syd Fields' seminars, or from their reading of Christopher Vogler's *The Writer's Journey*, which in turn was informed by Joseph Campbell's book *The Hero with a Thousand Faces*. Read these books, take these seminars, and you'll find the notes more meaningful. Also, don't get your hopes up that these story consultants can or will get the script into "the right people's" hands for you. Even, or especially, if they claim they can.

Only show your work to people who can't hurt you professionally. Don't slip your less than perfect work to someone who works in development, even if they are a friend. And never ask them to give it to one of the company readers to do coverage for you as a favor. This spells death wish. Readers are trained to say, "No. I hate it," ninety-nine percent of the time, and "I actually like it," only one percent of the time. It costs companies less not to make a movie than to make one. This is why professional script readers, and their bosses, are too traumatized to like anything. Script coverage ends up in a file that is kept for a very long time, in case your script ever comes back to the production company, even in a revised form. The coverage proves that the time investment to read your material was already spent, and protects them from ever having to read it again.

Send the same company another script and they'll read their coverage on your last one first. Worse than points on your driver's license, these notes don't automatically melt away after a few years. Also, they don't stay in just one company's files. Assistants, even from competing companies, help each other out when they can. One might call another's company for the coverage on your script if they don't feel like reading it themselves. In other words, you'll have lost control over who reads your work, and exposed yourself to a paper trail of rejection that could haunt your script and you from here on. It's great to get feedback from a friend who is a reader, but not in writing.

Once you've chosen your reader, remember that he has agreed to look at your work, not piece your soul back together. Be clear with yourself and with them on what kind of feedback you want. You'll get the best notes if you give them your best possible work. If there are good reasons why the script does not represent your best work (i.e., your writing partner was hit by a bus before Act 3 was finished), it's OK to give your reader a small disclaimer, but then leave it alone. Your problems aren't their problems.

Once you've handed over your script, give your reader as much time as they want to respond to it. Don't ever call to ask if they've finished yet. Let them call you. If time is a real factor, say so when you give them the script, and don't hand it over if they say they can't look at it within your particular time frame.

Let them read it, then listen. Really, actually, actively, listen. This rewards your reader for the work they've done on your behalf, and encourages them to invest more time and attention. Take notes, nod your head. Don't interrupt. Agree with them if you can, and say, "That's interesting" if you can't. Try to keep a supportive face even though the anxiety or what you're hearing may be killing you. Remember, their job is delicate and difficult, and at this moment, they think it's harder than yours. Treat them like you believe that. People want to be honest but are often afraid to tell the truth because of your reaction, now or later. Especially if they have firsthand knowledge of how hard you've worked. Let them feel comfortable with how comfortable you feel.

If you must protect yourself from people's feedback, remember this: all speech has motivation. The speaker has reasons for what he's saying and why. These may not always add up to a pure, positive desire to help. Listen for his motivations. Listen for yours in response. If his intention is to emasculate for the fun of it, cut the meeting short.

Learn how to separate the identification of a problem from its solution. The former is the kernel of constructive criticism, the latter, the chaff. Your readers may not be great at telling you how to fix things but excellent at telling you what didn't feel right to them and maybe even why.

Don't ask, imply, or expect someone to fix the problems. It's enough of a service to point out what's weak, confusing, or emotionally dead. It's not your reader's job to fix it, it's yours. Don't reject a problem she identifies because you couldn't find a solution or one isn't immediately apparent.

Listen to the problems. Don't prematurely respond with solutions. This will let you hear what your reader is really saying. The goal is to identify what the problem is specifically. Premature "solutions" cloud this process. Solutions can be multiple, and it's easy to get confused following one, or another, right into another problem, then losing the way entirely.

Problems, on the other hand, are finite. From your group of readers and notes, you can boil them down to a single handful. While there may seem to be an infinite number of directions your story could go, there actually aren't. There really are very few ways for you to tell this story well. You'll know when you get there.

Realize that the problems readers find at any given point in the story might only be the result of an earlier unidentified flaw in the narrative. Try to identify at exactly which points in the script they began to have problems and look at the prior scenes for their root. If they don't think a character should make a particular choice, the fault lies in how you established the character earlier. If readers feel bored, it's because you didn't give your character enough personal conflict early on, and you aren't making their choices difficult enough. Readers and audiences will accept what you give them in the opening of the film at face value. However, they'll abandon their suspension of disbelief at the point in the script when you fail to follow the rules you've set for yourself.

After listening, and listening some more, don't be afraid to tell your reader what you don't agree with. Not for the sake of your pride, but for the sake of the film. Ask them for extra help and guidance in understanding their point if it's a problem you're not able to see. Don't make them falsely feel you're taking the solutions they suggest. They may look for them in later drafts or your finished film. Instead, show interest in their comments by saying how it helps you to identify the problems. Then, if you can, start to think out loud about other solutions their comments suggest. This will let your reader continue to invest in an ongoing dialogue that may indeed help you find a solution you both like.

Synthesize the feedback. If you've been listening well, after a few people have responded to your work you should be able to develop a pretty good sense of what works and what doesn't. More important, you'll begin to make out what the common points of confusion, disbelief, boredom, or excitement are. On the other hand, if you have not listened carefully, each reader's feedback will have been like a volley of isolated shots that you needed to dodge just to survive.

Realize when you gave your script to the wrong person, and move on. The wrong person isn't someone who's poor at helping. He's someone who deep down doesn't want to.

▶▶ 34. BRING BACK THAT LOVING FEELING.

It all started so beautifully. With the hope, promise, and excitement of a first kiss. Now you've woken up and smelled the dirty laundry.

Every stage of filmmaking requires a renewed commitment, tantamount to falling in love, all over again. Lose track of the spark of it all and you've lost the script, and the film. Not that you can't get it back.

As in marriage, you have to know when it's time to take some time off, go away on a special vacation together, or, alas, resolve yourself to an open marriage, separation, or even divorce. Here are some guidelines for what to do:

Take out that picture of the first moment you met.

It's a good idea when you're just starting a project to write yourself a note about what it means to you and save it in a sealed envelope to take out in moments just like this.

Take some time off.

You are mildly irritated with the characters in your script, and all you see are their faults. Recommendation: take a step back. Go off and work on something else entirely for a couple of weeks. Don't look back. At the end of the first week, have you found yourself suppressing a longing to open it and look at a couple of things? To make just one or two little pencil notes about a breakthrough idea or a bit of dialogue? Go ahead, but otherwise leave it alone. Absence does make the heart grow fonder.

Go on a special vacation together.

After the two-week break if you still don't feel any sparks or it's downright boring, try seeing it in a different light. Dress the plot up in some new clothes: change the locale, names and genders of the characters, and see if the story becomes even marginally interesting to you. If not, then maybe its underlying dynamics are boring to you. People who love the Romeo and Juliet story will go to see it told in a million different socioeconomic, national, and gendered versions. They are just in love with the essential tension of the story. If you're not involved with your story at this core level, then it's time to pass the script on to someone who can finish or further develop it for you. This is not defeat. This is being smart. This is:

Separation, or an open marriage.

Now that you and your script don't have an exclusive relationship with each other, it might be easier for you to get some perspective. Having someone else involved can help you get the distance you need to continue without feeling like your whole life is consumed by it.

Divorce.

But what if you can't find anyone you think would be a good match for you and the material? Say good-bye. Time is money and you can't afford to get bogged down. It's now officially time to cut loose from your little albatross. Yes, we know, it looked so cute when it was little and you guys had some great times together. You remember the times it really made you laugh, and how you would never have seen the sunrise that one morning if you hadn't been up with it all night. We know, we know. But you were different then, younger. You've grown, maybe outgrown, each other. You need the room for your new love. It's not betrayal; it's life. No one's wrong here. No one's to blame. You can always get hitched again some day if it feels right.

▶▶ 35. CUT THE MILLION-DOLLAR LOCATION ON PAPER, NOT THE EDITING ROOM.

Here's a nightmare for you: you are on the set, and all of a sudden you realize that this huge ballroom scene for which you have amassed a hundred extras in Elizabethan gowns could have been a reaction shot on the actor who witnesses it.

No one goes to a movie to watch a location. You don't walk out quoting a location's witty line to your friends ("and then, when the nuclear submarine said . . ."). You don't line up to see "that new mansion movie" the day it comes out.

Years later, when you're remembering a scene in a movie that moved you, it has nothing to do with the location. Just like your favorite, pressing memories, it's moments between people we remember. In film, these intimate moments most likely involve close-ups that could have been shot anywhere.

Filmmakers think they're being original when they claim that the location in question functions as a character in the story. It's an expensive cliché. For anyone or anything to be a character, it needs to have will, autonomy, desire, and the potential for change. How many ballrooms can you say that about?

The only movies we can think of where the locations truly are characters:

- The hotel (including the maze) in *The Shining*
- The fields and the house in *Days of Heaven*
- The house in *Psycho*
- The mansion and gardens in *Last Year at Marienbad*
- The forest in *The Blair Witch Project*. And that was cheap: it was nature.

The reason the money you spend on a million-dollar location doesn't often make it to the screen is that it is often cut, and rightly so, in favor of moments that advance the story. It's hard to get a performance out of an inanimate space. Seriously, it's difficult to control any setting well enough to get the beauty-magic-wonder-ominous-ness out of it. Especially when you're hyper rushed because there's an owner standing by to make sure you get out when you promised.

Don't forget that just as the rich tell us it's expensive to be rich, fancy locations come with extra costs. You can't dress an expensive set with cheap furniture. Big windows need big drapes. And they cost much, much more to replace than small ones do if your lights set them on fire. Rich people stay that way by paying attention to what things cost. If you scratch the mahogany floor, someone will notice. You'll be stuck with a bill not for floor polish but for replacing that entire section of floor. By the best floor replacers, naturally, and with the best old-growth mahogany, of course.

Remember that Shakespeare performed all his plays at the very same location, the Globe Theatre, without any change of scenery. Write the key scenes for your actors, and relax about the locations. Remember that spectacle can be as small as an actor lifting his pinky. On a fifty-foot screen, that's a big pinky. More may be more, but less in film is usually a lot more than you're used to.

Necessity can mother the invention of greater precision in writing your scenes or planning your shots. You can also fall back on these tricks:

- Rely on shots of exteriors to establish a location without the cost and hassle of actually shooting a scene there. Plan shots of the location without characters and action (like the establishing shots of Tom's Diner in *Seinfeld*), or make the action extremely simple. Don't plan dramatic scenes in these places because you'll have a lot at stake to get it right and you won't be able to afford the time there to do it. The rush will make you miss the scene's point, and if this happens, you probably won't be able to use any of it.

- Use still photos in a dissolve sequence. This can be used to establish a world of the past, as is often done in documentaries. Chris Marker made brilliant use of this technique to establish a mysterious, timeless future world in *La Jettée* (the film that inspired *Twelve Monkeys*).

- Use stock footage.

- Use dialogue, or voice-over, to establish a (prohibitively) lush location. Let the audience's imagination create the beauty for themselves.

- Nature is a million-dollar location that's free for anyone. It's also camera ready—already dressed. You won't need to change a thing. A desert's a desert. Snow is snow. And they look great.

- Arrange to use a location parasitically, on the day when other elaborate action is planned. You can add production value for showing up to film at the right time: a dirt track when trucks are racing, a school when kids are leaving for home in droves of buses, a gallery the night of an opening when the crowd doubles as some very well-dressed extras. If a location costs a bundle to rent for you alone, it can cost a fraction if you arrange to pay a "sublet" fee to other scheduled users for your brief stay.

6

SULTANS, DENTISTS, AND UNCLE AL

▶▶ 36. FINANCING IS NOT A CONSPIRACY.

The main point of the next few sections is to reveal the big mystery about where the money comes from. The answer is simply: wherever you find it.

Every visiting filmmaker guest at our schools was basically bombarded with the same question: "How did you get the money, dammit?" Asked aggressively, with the authority of a stick-up. As if the poor guest knew the secret and refused to give it up. Don't underrate your intelligence: if there was a single, straightforward answer, you would know it. The guests' answers, of course, were always different—some new and personal combination of hard work, persistence, and timing. Each answer a one-off solution: useful philosophically but practically useful only if you managed to decipher parallels to your case.

A million dollars is a million dollars. Four million is four million. How do you get your hands on a million dollars in the real world? No easy feat. You must therefore make your film an investment that promises to make back all that money and more. If you can't make a case that can convince a production company, a studio, or a junta of private investors, you'll need to find room on your credit cards.

▶▶ 37. THINK LIKE THE BUYER, NOT THE SELLER.

Here's the potentially hassle-free way to "set up" your film: (a) have at least one very commercially desirable script; (b) get representation as a writer-director at a large agency based on this script; (c) get an agent at the agency to "package" your script with highly desirable "elements" (bankable actor-clients and renowned principal crew); (d) let the agent sell this "package" to a studio; (e) hope that the agent can keep you attached as director; (f) collect the check, and prepare not to have any further financial or creative control—whether or not you are the director.

For the rest of us, what follows are the more circuitous (but perhaps no worse) paths to getting financing for your film. The best way to convince someone that investing money in your film makes more sense than burning those bills in honor of the gods is to convince yourself. Sales is the transfer of beliefs from one person to another. The best way to convince yourself is to do the homework.

There are no guaranteed ways to make money with a film, but there is a logic. The key is to plan your film in terms of the intended buyer (the end point) and work backward.

Say it's a teen horror film. Go to the video store and rent as many films in this particular genre as you can. Determine which company has made films that are most like your idea. Presumably, they're your intended buyer. The producers in particular are the ones you want to speak with. Look up articles about them and the production company in past issues of *Variety, The Hollywood Reporter*, and online. If they are an "independent" company (quite simply, any company that's not a major studio), they are most likely members of the American Film Market Association (AFMA). AFMA puts out a yearly directory of member companies, listing contact information and statistics on recent acquisitions and releases. You can purchase this directory from AFMA directly.

Between the information in the directory and articles from the trades, find out the following information about the companies you are interested in:

- **At what stage they tend to get involved (i.e., put up money).** Some companies buy only completed films; others will provide completion funds; others develop, produce, and distribute projects entirely in-house.

- **What films they bought recently and how much they paid.** Many of these companies make their purchases at festivals and film markets, so it's good to look at the trades published around the times of the most important ones, including: Cannes in mid-May, AFMA in February-March, Sundance in late January, and Toronto in early September. A full list of international festivals can be found in numerous places online.

- **What films have been their best successes and worst failures, both domestically and internationally.** Look in the trades, again, at the time of the film's release for box office information.

In short, think like an acquisitions person, and understand what they're up against. Everyone's afraid of losing their job. Your job is to make their job easy, by presenting them with a property they have every chance to make money with. Design your budget, write out your strategy for casting, for production values, and for scripting in a way that logically reflects their needs.

If you have no luck meeting with the acquisitions person or a company producer, the line producer of the film that most closely resembles yours may be easier to meet with. Line producers are the operational backbone of a production. While they are not responsible for raising the money, their job is to spend it responsibly. They design the budget and keep the production on track (line item by line item, thus their title).

Track him or her down (through the production company is one way), and ask if they'd read your script and consider working on it. Assuming they are interested in being the film's line producer, ask them if they would be willing to:

1. Budget the film in exchange for deferred pay.

2. Contact the production company you found them through, and other producers they know, on the film's behalf.

If the line producer is interested in being involved in your film, chances are they would be willing to do both of the above. A respected line producer should be able to attract the attention, if not the interest, of producers they have worked with.

If even a solid budget and trusted line producer attached to your script doesn't lead to interest on the part of the production company, you can work on attaching other elements—namely cast. By this we really mean name actors whom the production company will consider bankable.

Bankability is not an abstract, subjective concept. The Hollywood Reporter actually puts out a list of stars, ranked according to their ability to attract box office and to ensure financing, in an online and published report called Star Power®. This provides rankings for a range of more than five hundred actors and actresses in key territories around the world. If you are a producer looking to increase the appeal of your film with a certain director, Director Power™ offers a detailed look at the bankability of directors around the world, as well as in key individual markets. The ratings are based on surveys from the studio and independent sectors around the world and include development executives, distributors, film buyers, financiers/bankers, producers, sales agents, and studio executives. They were asked about the degree to which the association of an actor/actress or director with a film can accomplish or contribute to the following:

- Ensure financing (total or partial)
- Ensure major studio distribution
- Ensure a film's wide theatrical release
- Open a film (to significant weekend box office) on the strength of their name alone

Resources like Star Power® can give you a good idea of what kinds of domestic and international revenues or financing capabilities an investor or bank might expect of films starring these actors. You can sell a film packaged with a low-ranked star as long as your budget is appropriately sized. Your star's price tag should also be in sync with the budget and your reasonably projected revenues.

Attaching cast is a powerful way to sell your film; however, attaching a star is a delicate matter. It can be a Catch-22. You usually can't get past a star's agent if you can't promise them that the film is (a) already fully financed; (b) the financing is not dependent on the star's participation; and (c) the money to pay the star is in the bank now.

Your best access to name actors these days is through their managers, now that managers have emerged as a new class of producers. Agents by law can't be producers of their client's projects. But managers don't fall under the same legislation. Mike Ovitz put his finger on this loophole, and now agents are switching to be managers so they can have the option of packaging, producing, and participating in the profits of their clients' work. They can help you break through the wall of "can't get the money for the film without the star, but can't get the star without the money for the film" because as potential producers they can share the profits the film might make. Reputable sales agents can also occasionally resolve the financing conundrum by soliciting verbal agreements from foreign buyers that if such-and-such actor agrees to play in the film, rights will be paid in a sum sufficient to meet the actor's price.

There's a reason why "pass" is the operative word for rejection and not "no." It means acquisitions people would be ready to look at your project on another round if something significant changed. A truly bankable star is worth calling them back about. Once you have a star in place, a sales agent can help you target your buyers and get you in the door with acquisitions people and lenders. You still have to sell them as well on the fact that your film is saleable, as they make a living only off commissions from sales.

If after all your tries the acquisitions person is still not your best friend, you still have the option of making your film with borrowed money. Banks are not in the business of investing (i.e., taking a risk with) money; rather, they are in the business of lending it. They fully intend to get it back, with interest. Your reputation, or how much they like your script, does not constitute collateral for them. They need something more concrete. Such as contracts with established, reputable foreign distributors who have agreed to pay you a set amount for the right to distribute your finished film.

Piecing enough of these "presales" agreements together as collateral will give you a shot at borrowing production funds from bankers like Lewis "Lew" Horwitz of the Lewis Horwitz Organization in Beverly Hills. Lew enabled the boom in independent filmmaking by pioneering the practice of lending production money against a film's reasonable expectation of *additional* foreign and domestic distribution contracts. Lending, in other words, to fill the gap between monies currently promised by existing contracts and the film's (larger) production budget.

Lew stays in business by managing his risk. He works with the opinions of only a few trusted sales agents, such as Kathy Morgan (Kathy Morgan International), who can reasonably promise him that the film's eventual foreign and domestic sales will more than make up the monies he's being asked to lend to fill the gap. To work with Lew, in other words, you need to work with a great sales agent like Kathy. To work with Kathy, you need to have a film package with a clear potential to sell internationally. A film package with, say, a truly bankable star attached.

Neither Lew nor Kathy can understand why filmmakers so often refuse to treat their film project with the same kind of basic logic afforded to any other commercial product. If, for example, you were going to manufacture a table, Lew says, you would estimate the number of eventual buyers and the price they would be willing to pay. From there you would determine if you could afford to make the table at all, let alone potentially turn a profit. Kathy adds that she's upset when she encounters filmmakers that would put their grandmother's life savings into the world's highest risk investment—without even a clear and reasonable plan for how they'll pay it back. A plan that would make as much sense to the buyer as it does to seller.

938. MONEY IS MONEY (YOUR DENTIST CAN PRODUCE).

Money doesn't have to come from a studio, bank, acquisitions company, or a card-carrying producer. Producers don't bless money and give it a special quality. Producers are producers because they have money or can get money. So can you.

Who do you know with money? This pool is broader than "what producers do you know?" Maybe your dentist doesn't know that he's got what it takes to be a producer. Namely, money.

You've figured out who has money. Now, why should they give it to you? Glamour isn't enough (even if your production had enough of it). Neither is playing the charity card. Any of this week's refugees or disaster victims make a much more compelling case than you do.

Larry Meistrich, the producer of *Sling Blade* and founder of Shooting Gallery, one of New York's largest independent production companies, demonstrated film investment to us the following way. He said, "Give me five dollars." We didn't move. He said it again, this time in a tone more like, "Gimme five dollars." "Why?" was our natural answer. "Because," he answered. We were still waiting for a reason. "Because," he said, "I'll give you $7.50 back." Sold.

People will invest (notice, we didn't write "give" or "lend") money because they expect to get it back and then some. Larry built his business on the idea that investors get their money back (with interest, at an attractive rate) and take their percentage from the film's first revenues, not its eventual profits (if any). The deals are structured to make investors' risk worth it.

Hollywood is notorious for having accounting procedures that hide any and all profits from anyone holding a percentage point. Your investors make your film happen, and you should pay them back first. Investors invest in businesses, so if you want their money, you should set up your film as one—the kind in which people can buy stock and participate in profits. The advantage of legally establishing your film as a limited partnership is that if the film does nothing but lose money, you (and whatever savings or good credit you have) legally won't be held accountable for unpaid bills. Once the project is completed, the partnership dissolves, unlike regular corporations, which can last beyond the death of their founders.

Since you are presenting your film as a business investment, you should also have a business plan. There is help, both from books and from professionals for hire.

Louise Levison, the author of *Filmmakers and Financing: Business Plans for Independents*, put together the plan for *The Blair Witch Project*. Since business plans are designed for private investors who don't work in the film industry, a large part of Louise's work is education. She gives historical background, from the financial picture of the independent film business in general, to the particular successes of the genre in question. She spells out, given current market conditions, how the film could plot a clear path to recoup its investment.

The business plan serves another function—it's a buffer in case things go wrong. It has built-in disclaimers. When Louise writes them, she doesn't make the picture look as rosy as it can, or as dark as it could. She chooses films with varying degrees of success rather than just using blockbusters to represent your genre. She spells out what they cost, who they sold to, and what they made. She signs off, and her signature states that the information is true to the best of her knowledge.

Keeping your shareholders in the loop is an important way to manage them through not so good times. When people are not updated on what is going on with a film they invested in, they start to freak out. Guaranteed. Being kept in the loop is part of the fun for them. Don't deny them this participation. They want to hear about all the festivals you just entered the film in, and what positive motivational thing some distributor had to say about loving the ending, or how the film is building or gathering momentum. Basically, they want to know that you're working hard on behalf of their money and on getting it back. Also, don't underestimate people's need for acknowledgment and credit. A newsletter is a chance to constantly thank everyone, individually, for what they have done and what they continue to do. Include the helpful notes or suggestions you receive from your investors whenever you can. It will encourage everyone to feel listened to and valued—for more than just their money.

This newsletter is the informal equivalent of your quarterly report to your shareholders, and you should take as much care with it. Indeed, taking on investors is like becoming a public company. They have the right to know how you spent their money and what happened next. Preempt their requests for information with your own carefully spun missives.

If the prospect of a pack of control freaks breathing down your neck, peppering you with phone calls at home, demanding to know why you went over budget or didn't get the film into their town's film festival sounds like the nightmare that it is, then maybe the private investor route is not for you. Don't forget that if you don't structure your deal properly, investors can pull the plug on a project if they don't like the way things are going at any given point.

Don't go into production, for instance, with backing from an investor who agrees to give you only a certain amount of money up front, promising to funnel the rest to you as the production unfurls— or not, as the case may be. Even the best-run film productions can look like chaos to the uninitiated. That angel investor might get cold feet halfway through the production and decide not to give you any more money, causing you to have to shut down the shoot. Regaining that momentum later will be tough. Don't let one person have that much leverage over your project. As in all things, diversify your risk.

▶▶39. IT'S YOUR FILM WHEN YOU PICK UP THE BILL.

When it comes to tricky artistic (read: financial) decisions, an underlying logic applies: who paid.

You want to make this cut, the producer doesn't. Guess who paid. You want to use this song, the producer doesn't. Guess who paid. There can be lots of talk about the director's vision, but in the end, the film belongs to the person who put down the most cash.

On the set of our first professional production, we spent one half day arguing with the producers about a wig, another half day "discussing" a pink light filter, and nearly a full day "debating" which direction an actor should walk in from. As ridiculous as these arguments seem in retrospect (and believe us, they do), the truly embarrassing thing is that we thought we could win them.

At some film schools, if you use the school's facilities or equipment (even just a light stand), you have to sign a paper saying the film is theirs. This means they get to keep the negative, and if they want you to reedit the film before a screening, you will. Or someone else will for you.

"Rebecca" won the chance to direct an autobiographical documentary at one such film school. When she disagreed with the shape the editors' cuts were taking, they literally kept her out of the editing room. When she asked the school to intervene on her behalf, they wouldn't. Even though she had initiated the project, written the treatment, prepared the budget, made the pitch, and won the chance to direct it. Even though the film was about her family, featured her family, and was mainly filmed at her family's house. The school argued that it was their film. There was very little she could do.

No one wants you to experiment with their money. When someone reads your script and gives you money for it, it's because they've seen the movie—in their mind. Shot by shot, exactly. And it was great.

It's when the dailies come in that they may realize they see another movie than you do. In which case, they will feel confused and betrayed. They'll say you made a different movie, even if you made exactly the movie you wanted to make.

You've felt this way when you went to see a movie adapted from your favorite book. "They didn't get it right." Maybe they did, as far as they're concerned. It's just that it wasn't the movie in your mind, and you feel cheated.

The good news is that if you're paying, you won't need to protect anybody else's vision (i.e., money) but your own. If someone disagrees with you about how something's supposed to look, you can listen, but you don't have to negotiate. If you make a mistake, you'll literally be the one paying for it. There's a huge luxury in paying for your own mistakes, and terrible agony involved in having someone else pay for them.

So how do you make a film with your own money? It's a question of expectations.

If a short film or video project is what you have in mind, you can make one with the money you save from an extra temp job. On the other hand, a small, self-financed project may not be your idea of a film. Big, Hollywood, studio-financed movies may be the only ones that count for you. That's fine. Just remember that when you convince someone else to pick up the bill for your film—or even just part of it—you won't own it anymore.

When Rebecca was kept out of editing her film, she made a copy of the video footage and reedited it herself. The school-sanctioned editors' version screened once at school. Her version won the student Academy Award.

While we'd like this to be the happy ending to this chapter, we have to add that the story doesn't end here. The creative and financial decisions don't stop when the film is finished. They continue through the film's marketing strategy and its distribution—forever. Because the school legally owns the film, Rebecca had no authority to negotiate for the distribution strategy she believed was appropriate in order to bring the film to its intended audiences. Nor has she enjoyed any share of its profits.

Film students who haven't made films yet don't necessarily

know what it means for someone else to own their work, both creatively and financially. They are not necessarily emotionally prepared to accept the premise that despite how much they put in, in terms of blood, sweat, tears, and cash, the school's contracts may be written to maintain full and total ownership of their films regardless. And maybe they—or you—shouldn't have to accept such a price. It is a high one. If you are considering film school, be sure to ask what their policy is toward ownership of students' work, and be sure to ask yourself how you feel about it.

▶▶ 40. NO ONE CARES ABOUT THIS FILM LIKE YOU DO, SO GET USED TO PRODUCING.

Producers don't usually have all the ingredients together at any one time to make a film. As an artist, you do. You can satisfy yourself with the materials at hand and, once your creative work is over, sell the result. Producers, on the other hand, are always at the mercy of other people. They must rely on other people to do the creative work and on other people's money to make the film. They try to cover their bases by developing several things at once.

Your film won't be the only film a professional producer is working on. Especially in this age of multiple producers, producers will take on more than one project at the same time and wait and see which one they can snare funds and resources for first. The shoot date for that project will then move up while yours languishes in a corner waiting for that producer to come back to it.

The important thing to remember is that just because your producer is out on half-time producing a Star-Kist commercial in New Zealand, you still have a film to make. Ultimately, it's your film. No one else will care as much as you do whether it lives or dies. You are the single mother of the film. Men may come and go, but your allegiance and responsibility will stay with your child.

▶▶ 41. THE WRONG MOTIVATIONS.

If your producer is working on the film for a reason other than love of the script, he probably won't make it to the end.

If not for love, then the motivations left are: power, self-esteem, a sense of identity, recognition, respect, or money. If someone wants these things, it means that they lack them. Which means they won't have them to bring to your film and will look to get them on your production.

It gets worse. If someone lacks, say, power, the lack is familiar and, in this way, comfortable to them. In times of stress we revert to the most familiar behaviors. The person who lacks power will, at the key moment, choose to be powerless. Worse, people with problems often *create* problems in order to feel at home. Their problems then become your problems.

"Trevor" directed a film school project about a father-son relationship played out in a used car lot. The used car lot was naturally critical to the shoot, and his producer was doing little to find the location. So Trevor took on the producer's role and found the location, negotiated the price, hours, and other details himself.

On the first day, the car lot guys changed their mind and told Trevor's producer they couldn't shoot there. The producer's response: "OK, then I guess we can't shoot here." Wrong answer. Trevor became the producer again. He told the crew to keep setting up the next shot and stayed in the office with the car guys, negotiating until he got a couple more hours. He went out, shot the scene that was up next, and while the crew was setting up the next shot, he reworked his script to a story that could be filmed in one tenth the number of hours. When his two hours were done, Trevor told the crew to set up the next shot and went back to the lot owners. He got another hour out of them. And so on and so on until he made his day.

The lot owners were so impressed with Trevor's determination and chutzpah under the circumstances that not only did they let him finish his day there but they let him come back the next day to shoot what he didn't manage to squeeze in. Meanwhile, the producer sat on the sidelines, eating donuts in his car, choosing power-lessness.

How to separate the victims from the victors? Interview, hard. Don't be flattered and blinded by your excitement that someone wants to work on your film. Your job is to identify the real reason they want to work on it.

We've listed the wrong answers already. Your film should not be their route to personal growth or the shortcut to a career. They should love the film and feel they can make a valuable contribution to it. They should look forward to your film as a chance to enjoy the skills and confidence they already have. They should recognize in you someone who has equally high standards. Birds of a feather look to flock together. Someone with real skills and standards as a producer will look for someone to be an equally valuable directing partner. Someone who shares their standards, and who they know they can count on. Someone, in short, who has as much to give as to receive.

In short, leadership (the true, humble, and effective kind versus the dictatorial sort) is what you're looking for. In the interview, ask for case studies of conflict situations: times when they were involved in a conflict between two people, when they were one of those people, when one of those people was a stranger, a landlord, etc. Listen to how they handled the conflicts. In particular, listen for the magic words, "Part of it was my responsibility."

Leaders are people who take responsibility, not make excuses. Excuses are a giveaway that the person didn't feel they had, or currently may not have, power. People who take their fair share of blame are capable of seeing a bigger picture. They recognize that power and responsibility always go together, so that when you have power, you have responsibility to make things work, within your capacities. And likewise, when you take responsibility, you gain a certain amount of power. Leaders look for opportunities to take and manage responsibility knowing that even if this includes self-criticism, it also leads to power. People who take responsibility for a problem, in other words, intend to lead again. Without making the same mistakes next time.

The proper mix of taking responsibility and expressing power is important. Someone who takes power without responsibility is a dictator. Someone who takes responsibility without power is a miserable form of victim.

▶▶ 42. MOM, APPLE PIE, AND EXECUTIVE PRODUCING.

Parents of filmmakers, are constantly being tested to give financial, practical, and emotional support in large doses. Anything not nailed to the foundation of the house becomes a potential prop. Any room with an electrical outlet becomes a potential location. Any white wall can be painted. Any unused can of paint, tool, or old pair of slippers may be called into service at any time for their child's or any of his numerous friends' shoots.

We ask a lot of parents, and all they ask in return is for a little cooperation. Which is not a lot to ask. Your mother may be your most forgiving location owner and your most ardently loyal investor. Treat her well.

Tiare and Kevin's mother Michelle's garage became the unofficial prop house of choice for no-budget student filmmakers at both AFI and USC for five years running while they both made their way through film school. Michelle would sit in the dining room going through student loan bills as couches, chairs, and even stoves made their way from the garage, through the house, and out the front door on film students' backs like ants carrying bread crumbs at a picnic. A frustrated sigh once prompted Tiare to venture, "Someday this will all make sense and I'll pay you back and I'll start to make a living at this." "I know," Michelle said. And the wonderful thing is, she meant it.

After three years of seeking funding for her independent feature, an odyssey that took her from Miramax to Steven Seagal's art film production company (no joke) and back, Camille's mother,

Babette, stepped up as the *de facto* executive producer. Babette offered not only the Corsican family's home for the shoot, but also cooked all the meals with her sister, Sylviane, and got the whole village to pitch in with their homes, food from their restaurants, bread from their bakery—even pigs for background atmosphere.

Parents not only give in kind with homes, props, and emotional support, but many a parent has served as the first investor to put money on the table for their child's independent film. Scorsese's mother cooked, lent props, locations, and cash to let him make *Mean Streets*. Kubrick's first films were financed by an uncle.

Doing it "on your own" is fine in theory, but it doesn't usually work out that way for beginning filmmakers. When we asked Chris Eyre, the director of *Smoke Signals*, what was the differentiating factor between filmmakers who were successful out of school and those who weren't, he said: "The students that had good relationships with their parents were more successful than the students that didn't. Because they had a good relationship to authority figures, they understood that they had to be responsible to the economics of making a film, and consequently they knew how to handle their place in the power structure of working with a studio."

The economics of your first films won't necessarily make financial sense. Which is why it's so important to find investors and supporters motivated by more than financial return. Filmmakers succeed through their relationships. Sometimes the most important ones are the ones they have with their families.

7

IT'S THE BUDGET, STUPID

▶▶ 43. IF YOU DON'T UNDERSTAND YOUR BUDGET, SOMEONE WILL MISUNDERSTAND IT FOR YOU.

Think the budget is for producers?

A budget is a blueprint of priorities. It tells what you want to spend on what. Behind every "what" and "how much" there should be a very good "why."

The "why" should come from you. You must now look at your script as a director, not as a writer. If you have until now been laboring to bring the script to term, this part can be hard. But now your script-baby is out there on the delivery table and you must raise it to live up to the celluloid destiny you know it has.

What does your script need most urgently to come to life—red blooded and standing on its own two feet? Your budget is like Dr. Frankenstein's manual. The particular combination of line items will result in bringing to life either a monster or something more manageable.

Because no film, regardless of scale, ever has a big enough budget to cover everything, every item you spend money on takes money away from something else. Spend money on the monster's costume, and you may leave out its heart. Would you leave this kind of decision to someone else?

Budgets are not mysterious. They're just tables of what things cost multiplied by how much of them you need. Change any of the assumptions (number of crew, actors, locations, shooting days) and the budget changes. Study budgets of student films at film school libraries (call ahead) and independent features at the Independent Feature Project's (IFP) library in L.A. or N.Y., and at the Academy of Motion Picture Arts' library in L.A.

When you read the budgets, don't just see numbers in columns and dry notations sitting stiffly on paper. See the movie. This is an especially helpful exercise to do with movies that you have seen and can recall. Train yourself to look at the budget and extrapolate its ephemeral result.

As a director, you want to know the budget better than the producers do, so that you can be sure that your money is spent wisely for the film (if it's your money), or so that you get what you want for the sake of the film (if it's their money).

When it's time to cut the budget, your understanding of what things cost can have you either making the wisest choices (cut locations, not crew members) or making smart changes to the script that result in better budgeting (combining two scenes, rewriting a scene as voice-over, replacing a live-action flashback with a number of dissolving stills).

Overall, the best budgeting strategy is to maximize the time you have on the set. That's where and how you'll make the film. By having the time to shoot it. Since you don't have enough money, give yourself and your crew enough time to make use of what you have. Time also allows you to spread out the work more reasonably. Shorter days (twelve hours versus fourteen hours, for example) do wonders for the mental and physical health of the crew, giving you a better work environment and a better film.

▶▶ 44. DON'T HIRE SOMEONE ELSE TO TELL YOU HOW TO SPEND YOUR MONEY.

A producer in the real world is someone who finds the money. That person has every right to the credit cards. Real-world producers hire the director. The director can spend money only with the producer's knowledge and approval. The director is an expense. The director can be fired.

It's the reverse in student filmmaking and much of independent filmmaking. These films are "director-driven." Meaning, there's no money, and the only thing that's driving the project, really, is the director's obsession (and money). The director "hires" the producer. Like everyone else, the producer is "hired" for free.

As long as the producer does not bring in money, he or she is the director's employee. This emasculated producer, hired by the director for free and told what to do, can tend to act out. With no creative control and no financial leverage, these producers—be warned—can resort to spending. Spending money is their shortcut to the illusion of power. It's the angry Beverly Hills housewife syndrome: revenge by plastic. It sabotages the production, sometimes intentionally. A friend, whose name we won't use, was shocked to turn around to face his producer's $60,000 spree. For the sake of the production, so-called, but really more for the guy's ego.

Even if it isn't malicious, someone who doesn't know the value of money is less likely to appreciate what things really cost. There's nothing easier than spending money. It's something else to earn it, or negotiate it.

The biggest thing to remember is that it's not the producer's job to spend money. It's the producer's job to spend wisely. Not just money but resources in general, which include people, equipment, and locations. Producers should allocate your production's resources and assets in a way that will maximize their use, thereby producing the best film possible.

You want a person who is a good communicator and ally and who knows that she or he can sit down with you and rationally discuss the best way for everyone to get what they need to make the movie work. This person will have to negotiate not just with you, but with your crew heads and investors, repeatedly, as the film's needs evolve. Producers negotiate not just for money but for other means, ways, methods, consideration, leniency—whatever the production needs.

And it will need. And need. This is why you need a producer with the emotional and rational endurance to go the long haul with you.

Basically, you're looking for the kind of person you would want to go on an expedition to Mount Everest with. The kind of person who will trust you to lead and that you will trust to serve as your anchor. The person you would trust to hammer in the footings your life might depend on later. Who would share their oxygen with you if you ran out. Who would stop you from doing something stupid like climbing too high or too fast, and who you would believe, despite your altitude-induced delusions.

The best reason to hire a producer is because you need a partner. Someone to share, not assume, the decision-making responsibilities of the project. In order to be a helpful partner, you must be informed about each other's jobs. Don't hire one and say, "Just go do what you do."

Producers can save your life, ruin it, or allow you to ruin it. So pick someone you respect for reasons you understand, and make sure that person respects you for reasons you understand as well.

▸▸45. PRODUCERS AREN'T PARENTS.

Let the producers play parent and you're left playing the child, in your terrible twos. Typecast and inevitably dismissed, both by the producers and the crew, as irrational, spoiled, and egocentric. Your assertions will become characterized as "tantrums," not statements of reasonable intent.

It may seem nice to have someone providing milk and cookies, a warm blanket, and regular nap times. But don't eat the cookie. The dynamic plays into not only the producer's but also the crew's latent envy of the director. It manifests their quiet resentment that the director has been given the freedom to express him or herself while they labor to the service of the baby's whims.

The parent-child game gives producers and crew a false sense of power. It promotes the idea that the director has been given authority by them and keeps it only through good behavior.

Get a mothering boyfriend or girlfriend if you must. As soon as you make a producer your parent, you allow your relationship to revolve around a personal dynamic, not the professional one. Remember the distinction: parents nurture their children and offer unconditional love. Employers do not. Employers hire people to do a job. They fire people for not doing a job. As a director for hire, you will receive money for your work, not love. Don't expect anything else.

If you are launching an independent project and looking for a producer, look for a peer. Chances are neither of you will get rich off this film alone. Maybe you'll make a nice living if you can manage to work together as peers for two, three, or more films. Then you'll be friends, partners. Then people won't think of you two as the producer-parent and the idiot-savant director-child in film production day-care who gets unleashed periodically to play with actors and expensive toys, but has to be watched in case he puts something in his mouth and chokes.

▶▶46. YOU CAN NEVER BE TOO RICH, TOO THIN, OR TOO UNDER BUDGET.

The first rule of investing in the stock market: don't lose money.

The second rule: don't lose money.

In stock market investing, as long as you don't lose money, you're ahead. As a filmmaker, as long as you get your money back, you can make another film.

Naturally, with the money back in hand, you've got the means to start again. But there's more to it than that. To other producers and investors, to bring a film in "under budget"—regardless of scale—is an instant certification of trustworthiness. It means you stared into the future and got it right.

Set the budget at $1,000 and make the film for $800 and you've won. Much more than $200 or $200's worth of prestige. Because it's so much easier to spend money than to save it, coming in under budget reflects a combination of careful advance planning and judicious on-the-spot decision-making.

The future is always unknown. Just as a business that can project its earnings with accuracy gets points on Wall Street, the film-maker that can accurately predict a budget and then outsmart it holds the keys to the future.

▶▶47. MAKE SURE YOUR SHORT FILM IS SHORT.

Don't give your short film an inferiority complex by trying to make it something that it's not. Like a feature. Squeezing the feature's traditional three acts into three minutes is not always a good idea.

Likewise, making the film longer just so it can be taken more seriously is faulty thinking. A mediocre twenty-seven-minute film is in *no* way better than a good three-minute film. Especially to the people who watch them for a living. That is, the very people your film will seek to impress. "One of our worst nightmares are those short films that want to be features," says David Russell, president of Big Film Shorts, a short film distribution company. "Invariably you can tell that story in five minutes' less time. Cut those five minutes and you'll have a better time selling it, and it'll be better filmmaking."

A film should be the length it needs to be, but shorter if at all possible. "Too long" is a complaint heard more often than "too short." "I'm from the make it ten minutes or make a feature school," says producer Kim Adelman, a founder of FXm Shorts, the Fox Movie Channel's effort to produce original short films. "Why spend all that money if you're not going to sell it? There's a myth that if it's thirty minutes long HBO's going to buy it," she says.

Even if it does sell to HBO, longer films won't necessarily score any more money than shorter ones. We've heard that Sundance Channel/Showtime won't pay more than the low four figures to license a short—regardless of length—for two years of unlimited TV distribution. Most distributors that pay for short films pay the same flat (and very modest) fee regardless of length.

A five-minute film can teach a lesson, sometimes comically or poignantly. It can share a moment, possibly, even in real time. Short films are memories, jokes, questions, lessons, and anecdotes. Many of the tightest ones can be described in one sentence. Short films are a snapshot to a longer film's photo essay. But sometimes snapshots are the most revealing of images.

A single song can be as complete an artistic whole as an album. A poem is short, but that doesn't necessarily make it less powerful than a novel. Short becomes part of its strength—an asset to its decisive tone or to its mysterious beauty. The challenge is to try to understand what a short film can say that a longer film couldn't. Or, in any case, how a short film can say something differently.

Without commercial outlets for short films, television commercials offer some of the best and most accessible examples of how much can be achieved by respecting the short form. As a small girl pulls petals off a daisy one at a time, a grave voice counts down the launch of a nuclear bomb. As the camera moves in closer and closer on her face, an atomic bomb explodes and we see a reflection of a mushroom cloud in the girl's eyes. These understated yet explosively powerful thirty seconds created by Lyndon Johnson's presidential campaign against Barry Goldwater in 1964 are still seared in memory despite the fact that the spot aired only once before an emotional audience response got it pulled. Just thirty seconds at a time have succeeded in getting a generation to want to give the world a Coke, and you to wonder if you've got milk.

▸▸ 48. THE $60 FILM.

It's just as easy to fall in love with a cheap film as is it to fall for an expensive one. Maybe easier, because we are generally predisposed to lend a sympathetic eye to the underdog.

These are some of our favorite films, all potentially made for the cost of some three rolls of film plus processing (if you use Super-8, this adds up to $60). None of these films attempts to cover up or apologize for their low budgets. They either hold out their budgetary limitations as a testament to the urgency behind their need to share their passion for the material, or treat the micro-budget as a negligible fact that has no effect or bearing on the work.

1. *Sour Death Balls* by Jessica Yu. Approximate cost: $60.

   A bunch of kids and grown-ups try keeping this incredibly sour candy in their mouth as a fixed camera records their tortured expressions and a fabulously appropriate rumba score keeps the beat. Under ten minutes, the film got into Sundance and won the hearts of executives at Fox's F/X network, who offered Yu the opportunity to direct a longer short for the network. That short was also well received and screened frequently on television and at festivals, generating tremendous word of mouth for the filmmaker and cementing her career launch as a director.

2. *Gerbil Trilogy* by Alyssa Buecker, age fourteen at the time. Total cost: possibly under $60 for all three films combined.

   Alyssa Buecker took her first filmmaking class at age eleven, the same year she acquired her first guinea pig, Hazel. At fourteen, Alyssa wrote, directed, and narrated a trilogy of films starring her (by then) nineteen guinea pigs, using her family's home video camera. Her work (*Hazel the Guinea Pig's Package*, *The Christmas Caper* [a crime-thriller], and *Guinea Pigs from Mars* [a sci-fi adventure]) won three awards at the Kansas Film Festival and was bought by HBO for broadcast on the network. HBO has commissioned her next project: *The Carrot Wars*, a *Star Wars* spoof. Alyssa says that the hardest part of directing her films was making sure the guinea pigs behaved when in front of the camera—everything else she needed to learn she picked up in the community class. Alyssa now teaches filmmaking seminars for children at the Lawrenceville, Kansas, public library.

3. *Blow-job* by Andy Warhol. Total cost: three rolls of b/w 16mm film, processed.

The film shows only the man's face, breathing heavily, with eyes half closed, shot from a low camera angle. The rest gets left up to your imagination as prompted by the title. As reels of film run out, the emulsion fades to wide. The camera gets reloaded, over and over again, until the guy—or the audience—decides the guy has come. This simple film draws its power from implying our direct participation in the actor's arousal. No special effects, dolly shots, or even camera movement were required to achieve this—only a choice of camera placement.

4. *Blue* by Derek Jarman. Total cost: over $60, but you can do it for less. The film served as an emotional catharsis for Derek Jarman, an HIV-positive artist and filmmaker, at the end of his life. The film is nothing but a 35mm blue screen, echoing with a rich soundtrack of voices and meditation. You can make your own version—say, in yellow, with your camera turned to your kitchen's wall and your friends providing the audio on subjects of importance to you and them.

▶▶49. FILM VERSUS VIDEO.

The wrong question: "Which is better?" The right question: "Which is better for this story?" If you had to ask us, film will always *look* better—mysterious, luminous, magic. Film's way of recording light—on emulsion—thrills us more than the way information gets recorded on a magnetic band or a computer disk. But beauty isn't everything, and sometimes beauty is counterproductive to a story.

Every medium carries the cultural messages that have been assigned to it. TV news is shot in Beta-cam video, and therefore Beta-cam video sells a "TV news look." By corollary, it also conveys the associations we have toward TV news: that it's real but maybe exploitative, uneven, spontaneous, rushed, raw, and potentially soaked with blood. These may be the very themes you want to echo in your movie. Or they may not be.

Black-and-white 16mm film has the associations of early news-reels: including innocence and deaths beyond the reach of memory. Color 16mm is the stuff of the documentary revolution of the six-ties and seventies: the direct cinema of the Maysles brothers, the melancholy documentary odes to America by Frederick Wiseman, and the sweaty shoulder-held camera of *Woodstock*. Kodachrome Super-8 film has the fragile sweetness of past birthday parties and the shock of how young and wide-eyed and maybe even sexy your parents looked. Hi-8 video carries the baggage of the Rodney King tape and your cousin's bachelor party—fast, cheap, and out of control.

The Blair Witch Project and *Celebration* stand out for their abil-ity to link story to medium. Both were shot (largely) on digital video, and neither should have used anything else. In both cases, the video lent the message of unmediated reality, garish immediacy, and unnerving intimacy. Film, with the time it requires in lighting, setup, processing, printing, and projection, sets a distance in front of what's filmed. This distance is passed on to the audience and serves as a space for observation and reflection. Video gives no time or space to delay response. In the cases of these two "films," the col-lapse of thought and reaction time served the story.

Today's digital video, of course, offers a certain clear and pro-found advantage: you can afford it. Which is reason enough to use it. Peter Broderick, founder of Next Wave Films, a company of the Independent Film Channel which specializes in financing and pro-ducing digital video productions, notes that more and more film-makers are choosing to make films independently because they don't want to spend years trying to raise money. Money for which, in most cases, they would have to trade creative control. DV will allow them to spend a higher percentage of their time making movies instead of making deals. Although initially viewed as a low-cost alternative, established filmmakers such as Eric Rohmer and Mike Figgis are increasingly turning to DV for the creative freedom it allows. Broderick believes that in time the low cost and terrific mobility and ease of DV may actually evolve new paradigms for storytelling and producing, eventually making it the media of choice.

Broderick predicts that once filmmakers experience the degree of creative control and intensity offered by this medium, they will find it hard to go back to traditional forms—both of storytelling and of film financing. Certainly, once filmmakers realize that they don't have to wait for anyone's green light, they're likely to be less patient when a production company says no.

8

GET THE RIGHTS OR GET A LAWYER

▶▶ 50. IT'S PROPERTY EVEN IF YOU CAN'T TASTE, TOUCH, OR FEEL IT.

Intellectual property (including songs, pictures, signs, and a piece of writing) isn't something you can build a picket fence around, but it's property nevertheless. Like anything that belongs to someone else, you need permission to use it. Using it without asking them first is stealing by any other name.

We were at a panel discussion where a filmmaker asked if she should tell Nike that she had used their logo prominently in her film. "Maybe they'll pay me money," she said hopefully, arguing that it was some kind of advertisement. Not.

Beginners want to believe that their film isn't a real film and therefore doesn't have to follow the same rules. It's true that if your film screens for absolutely no one but your dog or people in your class, for all intents and purposes, it doesn't really exist.

But you shouldn't be making your work for the worst-case scenario—a show-and-tell for school. You should be making it for the best-case scenario—selling it or, in any case, screening it in a commercial venue. Some filmmakers settle for just the festival rights, with the idea that their film won't show anywhere else. And yet isn't the very point of festivals to get the attention of someone who can show it somewhere else?

David Russell, founder and president of Big Film Shorts, a short films distribution company, laments the number of films he'd really like to sell the broadcast rights to but can't. Because the film "borrows" someone else's intellectual property, without permission, the film is not entirely the filmmaker's to sell.

Maybe Shaun Cassidy's people won't sue you personally for the unlicensed use of his version of the Crystals' "Da Doo Ron Ron," especially if there's literally no money in your pockets. But say you license the film to David Russell, who gets it a distribution deal with HBO. HBO's got some deep pockets worth suing.

Broadcasters know they've got something to lose, and won't license a film unless their Errors and Omissions insurance policy covers it. E&O insurance covers them should the slighted owners of intellectual property come out of the woodwork and sue. Yet insurers won't grant the coverage without the full assurance from distributors that the film is fully cleared. David Russell doesn't want to be sued, so he makes sure you did indeed get all the rights before he touches your film.

Afraid those rights might cost something? Think it's extortion? Imagine what kind of leverage they'll have when your sound is mixed and you really, really need them to sign off.

Dropping in a Rolling Stones song to your soundtrack without the rights is a combination of stupid and lazy. Stupid because you will get turned down by the owners of the rights unless you can meet their price. Bill Gates paid more than a million dollars to use "Start Me Up" to launch Windows 95. Don't think that since you're not Bill Gates they won't ask the same of you. The point is, they can get a million dollars, so why should they give you the rights for free? Lazy, because there are plenty of ways of getting free and clear material.

▶▶51. MORE RIGHTS TO MAKE SURE YOU'RE NOT FOUND IN THE WRONG.

Artwork

Yes, that *Kiss at l'Hotel de Ville* poster popularized on freshman girls' dorm room walls is under copyright. Robert Doisneau took the picture, his estate has the rights, and you can't legally film it without their permission.

Alternatives to using expensive, copyrighted material:

- Your art director or an art student can produce a poster/painting for your use.
- You can rent cleared art from a prop house.
- You can buy "royalty-free" photographs and art on CD-ROMs.

Storefronts

If the camera dwells on it long enough for someone to read it, get the rights, in writing, from the owner.

Logos

Unless you have written permission, these must be "Greeked"—amended to the point that they can't be recognized as the brand in question.

Actors

Some schools have waiver agreements with actors' unions—SAG (Screen Actors Guild) and AFTRA (Associated Federation of Television and Recording Artists)—allowing students to work with actor-members at a nonunion rate (i.e., free). But this is only on condition that your film never makes any money. If you're working with a waiver agreement, read it. It may state that if the status of distribution changes—i.e., you make money—you're responsible for what it would have cost to hire someone for a paying project. SAG's minimum rates are $617 per day. David Russell of Big Film Shorts says this clause has kept some films out of distribution, because the money a broadcaster might pay wouldn't cover what the filmmaker would then owe the actors.

Random people on the street

People own the rights to their own image, likeness, and voice. They don't surrender these just because you have a camera. News reports are allowed to show people in the context of a news event (in honor of the public's right to know about the news), but that's only for a one-time broadcast. For subsequent broadcasts they need permission from anyone recognizable. Documentaries, which are designed to be shown more than once, need to get the permission in writing of anyone they show. If you're making a narrative film and want to include some of those regular people in your shot, it's the same thing. You must technically have the signed permission of anyone who could be recognized on film.

9

HUSTLING

▶▶ 52. THE BEST PRODUCERS ALSO THROW THE BEST DINNER PARTIES.

Some of the best no-budget producers we know make working for them seem like a big party that you would pay to attend. They are good producers, because they know how to make everyone feel important, recognized, and well provided for.

At AFI, Michael Shuken was known for his ability to make every shoot, regardless of the budget's modesty, feel like a party. He gave everyone the impression that they were on a cruise, and this "effortless" graciousness was worth all the effort he put into it. Specifically, he worked at creating a sense of abundance. He started each day asking virtually every crew member what they wanted and what they needed. If it was at all possible, he did it. If it was impossible, he leveled with them and, with that person's involvement, came up with another solution. Michael was someone who made everything seem possible, because he (generally) believed it was. When people feel that their needs will be met, they don't feel as needy. When you know that there's food in the fridge, you can forget that you're hungry.

More secrets of hosting great parties (and film productions):

- Preproduction is the key to seamless execution. Make and freeze as much as you can ahead of time. If you have to do everything at the last minute, you'll be exhausted, irritable, ineffective, and probably burn something or someone (i.e., it's never too early to start getting your production elements in place).

- Clean as you go (i.e., deal with production disaster and personal conflict as it happens; don't keep putting it off until the situation explodes on you later).

- Everything should seem fresh even if it's canned (i.e., your poise in the face of disaster, your assurances to the location owner about your crew's trustworthiness, etc.).

- Don't let people seat themselves. You give them a sense of dignity and honor if you show them where to sit (i.e., choose your crew carefully and give them clear responsibilities).

- Don't have a centerpiece so large (think gadget, or set piece) that it gets in the way of conversation.

- Everyone's a valuable guest. Don't be rude to your guests, even the bores (i.e., be nice to productive crew members even if they irk you).

- Don't invite the bores over again (i.e., don't hire irksome individuals again if you can help it).

- Don't allow anyone at your table to speak to anyone in an offensive, hurtful way.

- Don't forget the glamour: make your guests feel that they're in the right place at the right time.

- Remember to have fun.

- Don't expect anyone to stay to do the dishes (i.e., the returns of miscellaneous props and equipment; dealing with lost or damaged locations, equipment, and props).

▶▶ 53. THE FORTUNE COOKIE GAME AND MAKING YOUR FEATURE.

Here's the original, restaurant version of the fortune cookie game: add "in bed" to the end of your fortune and read it out loud. You'll find that your fortune takes on a relevance and logic that it didn't otherwise have. The game works on the strange majority of them, whether the prophesy is "You will have good luck," or "You will soon see an old friend."

A variation on the game will help you get much more out of film school (and can also be adapted for your freelance filmmaking). Add "for my film" to even the smallest class exercises or weekend projects, and you'll make quick progress toward producing a polished film you can use as a calling card. With diligence and planning, you could even piece together a feature by the time you leave school.

Here are some examples of play, using one film school's curriculum as a starting point:

The fortune (a.k.a., the assignment) . . .	now, add the right attitude . . .	and the right magic words
First semester, you will make five Super-8 films . . .	which you will use as non-dialogue segments . . .	for your film
Second semester, you will make a five-minute b/w non-dialogue, 16mm film . . .	which you will use as a scene . . .	for your film
Third semester, you will prepare a pitch for a school-financed film . . .	whether or not you are selected, you will use this pitch while raising money . . .	for your film
Fourth semester, if your film was not selected, you will crew on someone else's film . . .	you will sign up for cinematographer, so you can use the better camera during down time to shoot footage . . .	for your film

The fortune (a.k.a., the assignment) . . .	now, add the right attitude . . .	and the right magic words
Fifth semester, you will prepare a pitch for a ten-minute dialogue film . . .	which will be a scene, or a whole sequence . . .	for your film
During every writing class . . .	you will concentrate on revising, polishing, and updating the script . . .	for your film
In every elective class . . .	you will bend the assignments to shoot scenes, and use the equipment during down time . . .	for your film
When meeting students whose work you like . . .	you will arrange to crew on their films if they will also agree to work for free . . .	for your film
When watching other students' films	you will take notes on who contributed money or favors, and who did great work, so you can call on them . . .	for your film

The premise of the game is that film schools offer any number of undisclosed opportunities for you to make your own films, if you play aggressively. The strategy can also work if you go to school on the installment plan, taking classes at a community college, one at a time, and on a need-access-to-equipment-basis.

To score like a pro, draw up a game plan before you go to school. Namely, have a script that you think can be realistically produced given the limits you'll encounter: unpredictable snatches of time, interrupted use of equipment, and inconsistent cash flow.

Here are some tactics that help:

- Write modular segments that can be shot independently or completely in a weekend. This will reduce the headache of re-creating a set to look just like it did in a prior scene shot on a prior weekend.
- So that you're not at the mercy of an actor's timetable, write a main character that can be played by your best friend, your gerbil, or yourself.
- Create interesting cameo roles to cast with relatively well-known actors or celebrities. Their names—even in small roles—will help you enormously in promoting the film to festivals afterward. Dan Mirvish got local and state audiences to line up for *Omaha (the movie)* by casting local celebrities, from a former TV anchorman to the governor of Nebraska. Keep the roles small so that an actor or other celebrity willing to make a guest star appearance on your show doesn't have to give you more than a few hours.
- So that you can shoot, or reshoot, at a moment's notice, write scenes that require no special props or equipment other than those you already have.
- Limit the recurrence or importance of a single character besides the lead or narrator. Coordinating reshoots or new scenes becomes exponentially more complicated the more people you have involved.
- Feature locations you have free and easy access to, such as your apartment, a public park near where you live, or, if you're a student, the school's buildings. This will give you a chance to shoot spontaneously, without extra negotiations, payments, permits, or travel time.
- Avoid writing children characters—the actors might grow up and change too much by the time you need to do a reshoot.
- Write as many nonsync (i.e., without synchronized dialogue)

scenes as possible. This will free you to take advantage of whatever cameras are available that weekend—sync sound capable or not. Also, nonsync shooting frees you from needing to record sound on the set, and is therefore faster and less expensive. Without the need for a sound crew, you can handle the shoot entirely by yourself if necessary.

- Feel free to rely on voice-over. It's easy to rerecord it if you want to change your story, or tonal point of view, as the film evolves.

Playing the "fortune cookie game" can become addictive, and that's not a bad thing. Even if you don't end up with a feature, the concentration will push you to work harder and smarter than you would have otherwise. You'll have more respect for the smallest assignments, the time you spend doing them, and your filmmaking in general. Even if the entire effort becomes a dress rehearsal for the more polished film you'll make next, think how much better that film will play on opening night.

▸▸54. FLIES WITH HONEY.

The saying goes: you catch more flies with honey than with vinegar. We're not sure why you'd want to catch flies, but if you want to catch favors, the rule is absolutely true. It goes back to another adage: nothing in life is free. If you want something from someone, you have to give something back. Starting with flattery.

Not the fake, saccharine kind of flattery that, while actually working to some extent, doesn't work as well as the authentic kind. Flatter them with your knowledge and appreciation of what they have that's special and what they in particular have to give. If it's money you're looking for, don't flatter their money, flatter *them*. For the ways they use it so judiciously, graciously, generously, and intelligently, to make the world a better place.

Another technique is to use the loss leader psychology: give away what you can. Scott Derrickson, the writer-director of *Hellraiser V:*

Inferno, who worked as a car salesman to earn money for film school, recalled this trick from his sales days: give the client a soda. When the client takes the drink, they feel psychologically indebted, on some subtle level. It didn't cost the salesman anything to give the client a soda, but it gives him a subtle upper hand going into the meeting.

Something you must give, or you'll go nowhere, is enthusiasm for your project, production, and filmmaking in general. With it you open the door for donors to participate, if only because they want to experience the joy and energy you have. The reason directors make such effective golden retrievers of favors and donations is that they are genuinely consumed with love and enthusiasm for their films. This gives them something to give, and it gives them a kind of confidence (as in, "I love this film, and I'm just here to give them a chance to experience the same joy. If they don't, or can't, that's their loss").

Whoever's going out on your behalf to secure goods, locations, money, and the like for your film should have this level of energetic joy, or they may do more harm than good. If they've got some joy or belief in the project but suffer from a little shyness, they can practice. Take turns practicing the pitch with the volunteer until you iron the doubt out of their presentation.

▶▶ 55. KNOW WHAT YOU WANT BEFORE YOU ASK.

People get nervous when you want something from them but aren't specific about it. They imagine the worst—because what you want could quite literally be anything.

Ask for something specific. By doing so, you eliminate the specter of the unknown, and everyone is much more at ease. You've put a specific proposal, need, or request on the table to respond to. They can simply say yes or no. No need to panic.

Asking for "help" in the general sense is the worst way to go about it. What is "help"? It's boundary-less. Help could be anything from becoming someone's mentor to lending them a million dollars or letting them borrow the car. Help is also a trigger word. People who stand at street corners use it, and so does that woman in the TV ads who has fallen and can't get up. In other words, "help" is a word used by the helpless.

Make clear that you are asking for something specific. People like to feel unique, so ask them for something that they and very few others could give. Sometimes people don't know what they have to give until you tell them. By paying such tribute to their particular qualities, talents, and resources, you'll make them feel rich.

If, on the other hand, you ask for something that many people have, they're likely to feel used. That obvious, generic request has been made too many times before. They've given for that reason already, sometimes to someone who didn't understand the full value of it. If this has happened to you, you know how annoying this is. Frankly, it's the way you feel when a drunk person kisses you at a party. You know it's not you in particular they're kissing. It's just that you happened to be there. It feels gross.

By asking for something specific, you focus not on what you don't have but on what you do have: a plan.

▶▶ 56. KNOW WHAT YOU CAN GIVE BEFORE YOU OFFER.

A negotiation requires give-and-take. Your first offer probably won't be your final one. Before you walk into a negotiation, know what you are specifically prepared to exchange for your specific request. Now phrase what *you* have to give in terms of what they need.

According to our one-time-car-salesman-turned-filmmaker friend Scott Derrickson, a salesman won't ask a customer what color car he wants. Instead he'll look at the cars he has on the lot and ask, "Which car do you like, the blue one or the green one?" This way he's narrowed the world of possible choices to the two he can offer. He has made his two cars, essentially, the only two cars to consider in the whole wide world.

Phrase your request in terms of what you have to give, therein limiting the entire world of potential compensation to the options you have: screen credit, an afternoon of your crew's hard labor to clean out their garage, a warm feeling, product placement—whatever it is you can do. This is to keep them from thinking about the world of possible compensations as such: namely, cash, check, or credit card.

Knowing what you have to give will also let the person you are dealing with know that you are taking the prospect of their donation of time, money, skill, and equipment seriously. There will already be a sense of momentum inherent in the fact that you have planned out what you have to offer them in return.

Don't make the mistake, however, of promising what you can't give. It will sabotage your future dealings. If it is a location you are negotiating for, you may lose the chance to go back there for reshoots. Instead of over-promising, feel confident giving value to what you can offer.

▶▶ 57. WHAT DO YOU HAVE TO BE SHY ABOUT?

The top five fears that keep people from asking for favors are:

1. "I'll seem like a loser for being in the position of having to ask for favors."
   Reframe this thinking as:

   • "I have the courage and motivation to ask for what I need to achieve my goals."
   • "I am mature enough to know that cooperation yields bigger dividends than trying to fly solo on everything."
   • "I'm looking for allies, not handouts."

2. "They'll think I'm crazy."
   Reframe as:

   • "I'm going to invite this person to share the joy of the absurdity. A chance to laugh about how ridiculous it is that I really need to borrow their lawn flamingo, and that I need it now."

3. "They won't believe me even though I will be telling them the whole truth."
   Reframe as:

   • "I'm telling the whole truth and can rely on my sincerity to convey this."

4. "I'm not telling the whole story, and I'm afraid they won't (or indeed, will) believe me."
   Reframe as:

   • "The parts I'm leaving out are truly irrelevant." (If this isn't the case, then you are lying and *should be* afraid to show your face.)

5. "They will criticize my plan or goal."
   Reframe as:

   • "I welcome constructive input because I am committed to my goal and success is my top priority."

▶▶58. SHYNESS WON'T GET YOU THE DONUTS.

Woody Allen said that over eighty percent of success is showing up. Go. In person. Or you won't get the donated donuts, or lighting gels, or vintage props.

Showing up means you care. It's easy to hide behind a letter or a phone call that you never follow up on. It's also easy for would-be donors to hide behind these: pretending they never got your letter, your call, or coming up with other ways to rationalize away whatever pangs of guilt your request may have inspired. It's harder for them to ignore you when you're standing there.

You get much, much more information about them in person. You can pick up cues on what they might need from you, and how to talk to them. Should you be driven and organized, talk fast, and promise to get out of their place quickly? Or do they kind of need the company and appreciate your taking your time? They will also get much more information about you, including a chance to sense, intuitively, that you're for real.

Case the joints in advance. Going undercover as a regular citizen gives you a chance to identify the nice manager and write off the ones who seem hassled and unhappy. Walking in with a relaxed smile for the person you're planning on talking to will help you feel welcome. An easy smile projects that you already like them, and helps them feel like they already like you.

Assuming you have the right approach, the person who's going to give will give, and the person who won't, won't. But there can be a middle ground. If someone says no to your first request, make them your ally in finding a solution. Ask, "Is there any way it could be possible?" and wait through the silence. They may try to fill the silence with a solution. Of course, if it's their solution, it's more likely to work.

A sense of humor at this, at all times, works. Feel free to share the joke, or charming absurdity of the situation. Of how ambitious your project is, and how small and underfunded you are. How even if it may not seem like a big deal to them, the fact that they can promise to give you a box of donuts on a given morning makes all the difference in the world to you. Not to mention their kindness, which really does lift your spirits for the next round of problem solving. When you thank them (in a handwritten thank-you note—don't dare flake about it), be sure to say how their generosity and spirit made you feel.

Know their business, and respect their hours and their needs. Don't ask a synagogue if you can shoot on a Saturday, or a church if you can shoot on a Sunday.

The only time the request by proxy (i.e., a letter-writing campaign) does work is when you're seeking donations from major corporations. Like Granny Goose, Inc., who donated all the potato chips we could load onto the bed of a pickup truck for a friend's film. Big corporations have a system for dealing with requests, which is a good thing, since it means they plan to give. Call up headquarters, ask for the standard procedure, and follow it. Just be sure to follow up and make sure that the right person got the right letter.

Since some corporations allocate a certain portion of their budget for tax-deductible donations, ask your school what their not-for-profit tax ID number is. If you are not in school, see if you can convince a nonprofit group to let you borrow theirs. In your letter to your potential donor, share that your project has tax-deductible status. In the all-important follow-up thank-you note, cite that ID number. The thank-you note functions as their receipt for the donation. Keep a copy for yourself and bring it when you go to pick up the donation. It will help the person who authorized it remember their promise and, in the more likely case, help the guy on the loading dock, who has never heard of you, to break out the potato chips.

▶▶59. SUCH A THING AS A FREE LUNCH.

On a student or otherwise no-budget film, where so many things can be borrowed or had for free, food can be the biggest budget expense. It's one you can't ignore (as in, everybody's got to eat). Indeed, good, hot, nutritious meals are something so fundamentally (physiologically and psychologically) important to a cast and crew that you need to pay good attention to it.

"Real" film crews call a caterer and let someone else take care of what amounts to a wedding buffet meant to last forty days straight. We're assuming you don't have the money. Here's what to do: think of it as one meal at a time, and remember that everyone and their mother knows how to cook something. From this reality checkpoint, consider the following options, each somewhat more convenient than you serving as your crew's short-order cook:

- **Find someone willing to prepare catered-style meals for the practice plus the cost of materials.** Someone from a community college professional food-preparation program or a fancier culinary institute. Look for someone with an entrepreneurial spirit looking to launch a catering business—say, with an entertainment business clientele. Promise you will recommend them to all your friends if it works out. Word of mouth is the best marketing tool a caterer has, and film sets are a good place to generate leads. If you can't find a cooking student, ask around among family and friends for a good cook who might be interested in trying out this career. Other leads can come from chefs at local restaurants and catering companies, placing an ad in a local paper, PTA newsletter, or food-related website, or even joining an online chat at one of the many cooking and domesticity sites.

• **Set a goal to get all your meals donated from local restaurants, one lunch at a time.** If you have an enthusiastic, likable person on your crew, put them on this assignment exclusively. Have one, and only one, person managing a calendar that they're booking with donations of free meals. It's embarrassing, and tasteless, to ask someone to donate a meal and have to go back and ask them if they wouldn't mind doing it for a different day because someone else is already donating that day. Lunch, served six hours after crew call according to union rules, is the most important meal of a crew's day. It should be hot. If a restaurant agrees to donate, ask them to donate this one.

• **Get breakfast for free.** Make a deal with one, or as many local bakeries and bagel shops as it takes, to pick up their day-old goods at the end of the day throughout your shoot. It will be clear to whoever's designated to do the picking up what kind of supplements will be needed to get through the next day's breakfast. That person should, if necessary, go shopping to fill in the gaps.

• **Work out a deal with the cafeteria.** If you're at school and shooting on campus, or if you're not but your locations are near a college, talk to food services. We were able to negotiate discounted coupons for all-you-can-eat access to the cafeteria for all three meals a day, along with a refund for tickets we didn't use. Some of your crew may be students and already on meal plans, which makes the deal even cheaper. There are two huge advantages to the cafeteria as caterer. First, it's open for a block of hours, meaning that you can call for meal break at the best time rather than having to coordinate a dance with the food's delivery (not too early, not too late). Second, while people will naturally make juvenile comments about cafeteria food, you'll know that (a) there will be enough of it; (b) there will be vegetarian options, including a salad bar; (c) someone else is cleaning up; (d) soda and coffee are included; (e) there's usually a dessert that people are willing to eat. One last bonus: if you're making a film at school, you can buy coupons for your picture and sound editors to keep them fed through the long days and nights of the editing process.

- **Put your friends and family in the kitchen.** Cooking a crew meal is a very, very tangible and meaningful way for your non-film friends and family to help your production. Offer them freedom to come up with their own menu and offer to pay for the ingredients. Try to coordinate the days you're getting home-cooked meals with days your location will have access to a kitchen (even if it's just for reheating). Reimburse them for the items on the store's receipt or, if you have time, buy the food for them (and perhaps other cook volunteers) in bulk.

- **Approach a supermarket to donate food or to allow you, on one day only, to buy products at cost.** Offer to credit them the full value of their contribution, along with the citation of a not-for-profit institution's tax ID number, in the thank-you letter. If you don't know what food you'll need, take advantage of this negotiated "at cost" day to buy bottled drinks, paper plates, plastic cutlery, tinfoil, etc.

- **Shop at restaurant-supply stores and other wholesale markets.** Certain wholesale markets are open to the public, but you can get even better deals at the stores that are truly open only to the restaurant trade. Call ahead to restaurant suppliers and ask about the possibilities of getting a one-day pass to shop at these stores. Also, city supermarkets get their produce from wholesale produce markets. The one in L.A. is downtown, on Broadway at Fourth Street. Pallettes are unpacked and the food is available for purchase starting at 4:00 A.M. Some will sell to you only if you've got a resale number, but most are happy to take your cash.

- **Don't think you can get away with having food on set just during mealtimes.** Film crews need food available at all times! People take out their stress, boredom, fear, and joy on food. Free-floating anxiety will set in if it's absent. Lights will start falling, film won't get loaded properly, people won't pay attention to their marks, and arguments will break out over ridiculous things. The general order and happiness of the set is a value directly proportional to the amount of available food at any given time.

- **Have snacks for every variety of food restriction or preference because they will all be represented on your set.** Your craft service table should be like a Benetton ad of culinary diversity. There should be something for everyone: the vegetarian, the vegan, the red meat-only eater, the nut-only eaters, the nut allergic, the tuna-only eaters, the no-tuna-is-dolphin-safe-antituna eaters, and the list goes on. The one group, however, to which everyone belongs but to which few will admit, is that of the junk food eaters. There should be plenty of food to satisfy every crew member's superego and id. Ignore one or the other at your own peril.

10

HYPE, FOR CHEAP

▶▶60. GLAMOUR IS A PRODUCT.

Hollywood doesn't inherently own glamour, it produces it. For other people.

One glamorous (although he didn't know it) executive we met put it this way. "It's a dream factory. Dreams are being *manufactured*. It's like when you work in a cookie factory, do you get to taste the cookies? Every once in a while. In this factory, every once in a while, we get to taste the cookies. Sometimes you get to take that cookie out to a candlelit dinner, to a premiere. That's where the cookie gets to meet other cookies. . . . But that's not your job. Your job is to produce the cookie."

Not illogically, the business is staffed by people who desperately crave glamour for themselves. People tortured by a simultaneous appreciation that glamour doesn't exist and by a secret, self-defeating conviction that it does—but just not for them. This is the sadness of Hollywood's slaves: they create beautiful Pygmalions, only to watch them fall in love with others. Rather than see that Pygmalion's allure was fashioned by her creator, Hollywood's most powerful persist in believing that glamour is somehow always for other people.

Your job, like theirs, is to create glamour. Only, you must create it for them: the executives, agents, and managers, who crave it most. Your job is to make them feel glamorous, or closer to glamour, by knowing you. Your means is to create it for yourself.

▶▶ 61. "STYLE IS PERSONALITY ON PURPOSE."

This quote courtesy of Raquel Welch via our friend Lisa Singer, who was for a brief moment her assistant. Maybe Raquel wasn't the one who coined this wisdom. But clearly she understood what it meant.

It's not just in Hollywood that no one knows anything. Everyone's existentially nervous, unsure if they're making any of the right choices. Make some clear choices and stick to them, and you'll seem as if you have found some answers. Making choices creates value. It's attractive.

If you're so-called not paying attention to style or personality, you're making a choice: it's just a sloppy, uninformed one that conveys you don't know what you want. It's impossible not to make a statement. Everything you wear, own, and drive is coded. Nothing is historically innocent. If someone saw a picture of you three hundred years from now, they'd know exactly when and where you lived and what you did. How you dress is like an address, a publicly expressed genetic code that tells people exactly where you live and what you do and how you feel about both.

Here's a good time to use the favorite all-purpose cliché: film is a visual medium. It's a series of visual choices, adding up to tell a story. What story are you telling? Refusing to make choices leaves your style and personality up to other people. Almost everyone on a film set has to make subjective decisions that affect the outcome of the final product on some level. Your choices should give them confidence that you know how to make choices.

Intention goes a long way. Make limits seem intentional and your choices are beyond reproach. Use the same logic for your film and you've given birth to style. Kevin Smith's *Clerks* wouldn't have been better if it had spent more money in production design. Same for Jim Jarmusch's *Stranger Than Paradise*, which made an elegant virtue of master shots without coverage. Goddard's *Breathless*, credited for inventing jump cuts, took brilliant—stylish—advantage of not having a sync camera or enough film stock.

Victims are the ones who have choices made for them. Make

your films and live your life in such a way that asserts that even if you had a million dollars, you would do everything the same way. Stop and recognize that you're on the wrong track if you think or act like anyone's style, or life, is better than yours. Start over. You'll only be a follower, and imitations are, by definition, valueless next to the original.

▶▶ 62. INVENTING CELEBRITY.

Unlike retail, film is a product audiences pay for sight unseen. You have to sell them the film before they have a chance to look at it. Stars are important because they are a known commodity and people will pay to see them. If you don't have any stars in your movie, you'll have to sell yourself.

If you're not a known commodity, you'll have to work on becoming one. You can. The institutions, emotional quirks, and built-in dynamics of this industry are on your side.

The studios used to have machines dedicated to creating stars, through underexposure. Giving audiences just enough information so they would want to know more. Hollywood's economy is information, meaning that its economy is fear. Everyone's afraid of missing out on the next thing. Profits—not to mention social standing—are made on the opportunity of knowing something before anyone else does. Being out of it has a high emotional price, too. Everyone's afraid of being left behind by the other kids. This is an industry driven by a raging fear of abandonment.

Use their fear to your advantage. Create a scarcity of information about yourself. Sound abstract? If you know anything about dating, you know everything about this.

You already know that hard to get is the only game that works. If you want someone's attention give them a little attention, but not enough. Try this at home. Think to yourself, "I have a secret," and watch your boy/girlfriend's response. "What? What?" they'll answer. Their need for you to tell them . . . what is, indeed, nothing, will grow manic. "What, what, what?!" They will start to fill in their own stories about what the secret is and why you're keeping it. You'll find their fantasies about the secret you're keeping to be quite interesting. As long as you keep the secret, you have power. Even when the secret is that there is no secret.

▶▶ 63. AND THEN GOD CREATED . . . *YOU:* TACTICS FOR SHAMELESS SELF-PROMOTION.

The goal is to get people to want to know more. But you have to let them know you exist first.

How to get their attention? We've broken it down in terms of getting attention for yourself and for your film, although there really isn't any difference.

Promoting yourself

1. Accepting the basic premise that there's no such thing as bad publicity helps you get used to the goal of publicity in the first place: people talking about you.

2. Act like you already have everyone's attention. Someone in the right frame of mind can make eating an orange seem like the sexiest act ever performed.

3. Start a rumor through the grapevine of producers', directors', and agents' assistants. Pose as a producer. Call up the agency demanding, "I want xxx's (insert your name) script." Assistants will call each other to get a copy. Your name will be on the radar.

4. Get a friend to call you at a restaurant, an airport, a meeting.

5. Get a conspiracy of friends to gossip jealously about you in bathrooms that matter: at premieres, film festivals, A-list restaurants in L.A. or N.Y., or, if you have friends on the "inside," at agencies and studios.

6. Have someone else return your calls. Possibly with the line: "Pat's not getting to her return calls today."

7. Learn from would-be rock stars:

- Call the cops on yourself.
- Send angry letters about yourself and your controversial work to newspapers, under an assumed name.
- Get a magazine or local paper, or a bunch of local papers, to write a human-interest piece about you and your struggle to be known. A strategy: get an aspiring writer friend to write it and to pitch the idea, as a freelance piece, to magazines. Look at the library's copy of *Writer's Market* to learn about how to go about this.

8. Learn from Spike Jonze, director of *Being John Malkovich*, an expert in the paradoxical art of anti-self-promotional celebrity:

- Send other people to interviews posing as you.
- Make it so that your publicity firm has to hire paparazzi to get photos of you.
- Go to interviews as the frazzled publicist who couldn't get you to show up.
- Hire your friends to act like strangers and beat you up during interviews.

Attention for your film

1. Create a scandal, a self-fueling news story. *Kurt and Courtney*, Nick Broomfield's documentary, became *the* hot film at Sundance the moment Courtney Love called the festival to threaten that she'd sue if they screened it.

2. Create an event people will recognize as the kind other people will be talking about, propelling them to go. If you can't swing an event, at the very least, throw a party. Amy Dawes, a longtime film reviewer for *Variety*, says it's amaz-

ing how journalists will respond to free food or drink. Screen your film to segue from the party.

3. Stolen from Jan Brady: make fortune cookies with fortunes relevant to your film.

4. Make a virtue of what you don't have (stars, explosions, elaborate sets, etc.). A Samuel Adams campaign uses this logic to sell its domestic beer against its imported competition with the slogan, "Never stuck in customs." For your film you might write a slogan like "No production value, and that's not even the best part."

5. Project the movie onto the side of a building at night (even if the police stop you—that can be a story in itself).

6. If you've worked with a record label to place music in your film, give out the CD for free.

7. Use Rave promotional logic: give away clues to where your film's party is, and keep it a mystery, revealed only to those holding the right "password object."

8. Have an actor or friend stand at the airport with a sign, either with a star's name, the name of your film, or both.

9. Have a friend run into a screening just as it's going to start and call your name, shouting that you have an urgent phone call from a buyer. Run out with the friend and pull the trick at the other screenings starting at the same time.

10. Plant an actor with a cell phone outside your film's screening room, pretending to be negotiating deals for your film.

11. Distribute flyers to local people beforehand in order to have a packed house. Make the flyers a different color so that if the room really gets too full, and a distributor is trying to

get in, you don't shut out the wrong people. Select local audience members strategically. Target those who are likely to come dressed like distributors (e.g., real estate agents, lawyers).

12. Leave cocktail napkins around festival hangouts, with "Bambi's" number scrawled on it (with or without the name of your film on the other side). The number should ring to a voice-mail announcing your film's screening times.

13. "Sell out" the screening by giving tickets to friends. Make sure you get everyone to know it "sold out" by getting your friends to stand in line, saying, "I wish I could get tickets to xxx (insert the name of your film), but they're sold out."

14. Hire actors (or friends) as stunt reporters to follow you around with a camera, interviewing you constantly.

15. Hire more actors (or friends) as stunt stalker-paparazzi whom you are constantly desperately fleeing.

▶▶ 64. DON'T BE AFRAID OF AGENTS, BE AFRAID FOR THEM.

You're about to pick up the phone to call an agent for the first or nineteenth time and you're nervous. Next to them, you have nothing to fear.

We each had jobs as assistants to talent agents before we started film school. In both cases we learned that agents' lives are the extended play, technicolor version of our anxiety dreams. A friend who was an agent at a top-three talent agency for six years recently reminded us that it's even worse than we remembered. To appreciate what it's like on their end of the line, imagine the following:

- You have two hundred calls to return, and another fifty to place.
- A client is calling for the ninth time to find out what you thought of a script you haven't read yet.

- A rival agent is having drinks with your best client right now to tell her what a better job he'd do for her.
- A client calls from the set to say that one cell phone isn't enough, and he wants another one for his friend. The other agents got extra cell phones for *their* clients' friends.
- Four lines are ringing and you can't remember who's holding.
- You haven't made enough money for the agency this year to pay for your assistant's salary, let alone yours.
- If you don't make more money soon, they'll fire you.
- Your third assistant this year is quitting. Your reputation is going from "difficult" to "abusive."
- Your new assistant is passing himself off as an agent and launching his own career.
- You're firing your fourth assistant and your reputation's about to go from "abusive" to "psycho."
- Your ex-assistant has become a big producer and won't return your calls.
- A client is complaining that $2 million isn't enough for two weeks of work.
- A client is having a nervous breakdown trying to get a grip on a two-line role and wants to know if you care.
- Your therapist is telling you that you're jealous of your clients.
- Your mother's hurt that she wasn't your date at Courtney Love's party.
- You're calling out your assistant's name when you have sex with your boyfriend.
- Another agent is taking credit for your biggest deal, and you can't say anything because he's a partner in the company.
- You're having a hard time coming up with inventive, original, and intelligent gifts for your clients' birthdays, anniversaries, shoot-start days, shoot-wrap days, and mothers' birthdays.
- Your gifts are not as inventive, original, and intelligent as your rival's.
- Someone who matters isn't returning your calls.

- You wonder if you're being paranoid, or if in fact, no one is returning your calls.
- You're wondering if no one's returning your calls because you've become paranoid.

Don't call until you've read this list enough times to understand that agents don't have time to hate you even if they wanted to. Read it until you feel sorry for them, possibly even protective.

Now make the call. Be grateful and polite to the assistant, whose job is even worse than the agent's. Ask for his name, and write him a thank-you note for anything he manages to do for you.

Leave a clear message. Calmly state why you're calling, what you have, and what you want. Call only if you have something they want, need, and can sell *right now*. If you don't, you're wasting their time. And they won't waste any more of it by calling you back.

▸▸65. GLAMOUR ON TEN DOLLARS A DAY.

Glamour is not needing anything. It's Lauren Bacall in uncomplicated slacks and a casually arched eyebrow. Marlon Brando with no more than a T-shirt, a curled lip, and talent. Not needing anything from anyone, least of all approval.

Falling in love gives you a shortcut to this kind of confidence. The "we have everything because we have each other" feeling. You do, until you don't anymore. Which is why we recommend friendship as a more reliable shortcut. With someone who can laugh at the same joke without either of you having to tell it. Who can share the joy or absurdity or sadness of any situation with you.

Because glamour equals not needing anything, it doesn't have to cost you anything. Love and friendship, the best sources of glamour, are free. And so are (or nearly) these other things, that will help you feel glamorous, or at least look it:

1. Always look like you're coming from someplace and going someplace.

2. Information is free. You can know about the best new restaurants to recommend to people you need to impress by reading reviews. You don't have to eat there in order to be able to use the name in a sentence.

3. It doesn't cost you anything to have an opinion. Since glamour is not needing anything, it also means not needing approval for your thoughts.

4. People give you credit for knowing a little about obscure subjects, so read art reviews.

5. It's not knowing people, it's what you know about them.

6. Keep the gas tank filled. You should feel you have a means to go anywhere, anytime. Freedom of movement is glamorous. It says you're in charge of your life.

7. Believe that there's nothing wrong with being poor. Especially as it's such a great thing to be able to talk about in the past tense one day.

8. Don't worry about not having a cell phone; it's too cheap a prop. People who have their assistants do the calling are the successful ones.

9. Only wear (and only buy) clothes that make you feel sexy.

10. Cultivate a knack for finding cheap things in expensive places. A cup of coffee at the Ritz is still a cup of coffee. Even if it costs $2.95 (the highest price we've encountered), this is still less than the cheapest McDonald's extra value meal.

11. Don't answer the phone, except between three to six A.M., when you have every reason to be home. And then only if you want to.

12. Remember that the real luxuries are the things you can't buy.

▶▶66. DRINK NO WINE UNTIL IT'S TIME.

You hear the cruel advice often: "Go to parties. Network."

Uncomfortable advice when you don't know what you're supposed to network for—i.e., what exactly you have to sell.

Until you have something tangible to sell, like a script, you're only selling yourself. This is nauseating, because it prompts you to attempt to be lots of things to lots of people, constantly trying to anticipate what they want, and then pitching yourself to fill this role. When you're selling yourself and you are rejected, the pain is a whole lot worse than when one of your ideas is rejected.

Write your script, or finish your short film, or write your movie of the week treatment first, then put your energy into trying to sell it. It's too much to worry about both at once. Save your energy for the work of writing.

While it doesn't hurt to meet people, it certainly makes a better first impression to say, "I just finished my script and I really like it," than it does to say, "I'm working on something." Wait until you're done: confident and happy with what you have, and you'll be in a much better mood and, therefore, position to sell it. You'll also enjoy the wine more.

▶▶67. IF YOU'RE NOT AT THE PARTY, THEY'LL THINK YOU'RE SOMEPLACE BETTER.

Whatever's in fashion is haunted by the inevitable visit of its demise: its opposite. Every "in" has a built-in "out." In Hollywood, the switch happens as quickly as someone thinks so. What's visibly prized is at risk, because it's about to be rejected.

No one ever feels that they're at the right party. Especially the person throwing it. Which puts you at a potentially better party until you step through the door. At which point you should remember to look like you just came from somewhere else. And on your way to someplace better. Hence, the "arrive late, leave early" concept.

On Monday, when people are talking about a party you didn't even know about, have your response premeditated. If you were simply at home with your cat Mothball, no one has to know. Say you spent the night with a special friend.

Unless you blow it and tell them otherwise, they'll believe that you were busy. You should think of yourself as always busy, so that the idea of going to a party is a rare luxury you give yourself. Indeed, it should be. If you're a filmmaker, then you should always be making films. Whether or not that means writing, or location scouting, or random driving to get ideas, or volunteering and working with a group of people who all figure in your script. All activities should relate to and reflect your commitment to making films, which may indeed give you someplace better to be than a party.

▶▶ 68. PARTIES: BASIC ETIQUETTE.

Rules of etiquette, like other laws, exist to protect people from each other. As applied to you, they protect hosts and guests from seeing you make a fool of yourself, insult someone, or drain the life and glamour out of the party with your fundamental boredom. Reverse the don'ts into the do's, and you realize that the logic of a party is to collectively make everyone else there feel good, and important. You're a shipwrecked group, trying to feel good about being shipwrecked together.

Getting dressed

Parties are definitely easier for the beautiful people. Examine *In Style* like it's *National Geographic*. If you still feel clueless, get a stylist. Really. Don't let bad taste ruin your chances of a social and, therefore, professional life.

A low-cost option is to find an underpaid salesperson at a retail store where the executive track shops. Pick one whose style is so great that in your best dreams of yourself, you would look like them. Ask if they would consider being your stylist. Usually they will be very flattered. This is actually what they are supposed to be getting paid to do for you at the store. But never mind. What you want is for them to help you, for a small fee, create the look with stuff from more affordable places. This is the challenge they themselves face, on their small salaries.

Showing up

Don't go to the party if you are feeling emotionally unstable or deeply vulnerable. If you must attend in such a state, avoid alcohol entirely, remembering that the morning after is the first day of the rest of your career.

If you're in L.A., a bus pass is like the mark of the beast. You'll never escape that stigma, so don't risk it. Get someone to drive you, or walk.

Don't go to parties where two people whose films you have double-booked (i.e., committed to doing at the same time) will be in attendance. Just leave the party if this happens. Double-booking is a common practice, and some say that you must do it to make sure you get on at least one project that gets off the ground. Just don't put yourself in a position where you're going to get caught doing it.

Conversation

Decide before you go what you are willing and not willing to talk about. Resolve what you want to share about your life at the moment, and what emotional sore or professional wart you'd like to keep private. Because the lines between professional and personal are so unclear in film, you may find yourself getting asked what feel like personal questions from people you really don't know that well. An industry party is not an interrogation room, and they don't have secret ways of making you talk. If you don't want to talk about something, don't.

As paranoid as you are about making yourself seem goofy and out of it, no one actually wants to see you weak. At a party you're only as glamorous as the last person you talked to, so let yourself be that glamorous person on behalf of the person you are talking to.

If they've managed to ask you a question you don't want to be asked, turn it back on them. "Actually, I'm so glad I saw you, because I'm so interested in what *you're* doing now." They may have been asking out of protocol, and will be delighted that you asked. If they're not comfortable with the question themselves, then you know you have nothing to be embarrassed about, either. If they persist in asking you an uncomfortable question, use the same strategy you used on essay tests: find a part of the question you can answer and respond to that.

Don't let anyone hook you in and make you an accomplice to a conversation bashing someone who is also at the party or whose friends are at the party. Run if someone wants to bad-mouth the host of the gathering and include you in on the conversation. This happened to us at a screening for a friend's film on a studio lot. A professor was invited by the gracious, soon to be very successful young director. That teacher spent a good part of the evening loudly deriding the former student for having the means to pull the film off. Envy can be a very ugly thing, especially after a few martinis. If you don't run fast enough in the other direction, you might be implicated when word gets back to the target. And it will.

Avoid making out at a party with someone you will work with soon. The rumor of this public moment of indiscretion will haunt you (ten-fold if you're a woman) all through your next job together.

Blowing the clambake
Leave, early.

11

FRIENDS, ENEMIES, LOVERS, AND THIEVES

▶▶69. SURROUND YOURSELF WITH PEOPLE WHO INSPIRE YOU.

Inspiration is not a moment in which you discover something new. Rather, it's a moment when you recover something of yourself. Of your own dreaming, energy, and faith. Of your own love, humor, and strength. When inspiration comes in the form of a film, painting, or song, the experience reflects back something that's already in you.

A friend is someone who can do the same. He can make you laugh because he already sees you laughing. She lets you feel strong because she already knows you are. Friends bring out the best in you, because it's what they already see. Surround yourself with people who are predisposed to believe you, and you'll be able to share what you believe about yourself. A friend helps you see the secret of your best self. No matter how successful you become, you'll always need a true north.

Sometimes people get the impression that they need to surround themselves with people who challenge their feelings of self-worth. They believe that somehow this will toughen them or make them work harder at being themselves. All these "challenging" people do is symbolize your own self-doubt and keep it at the forefront of your waking hours. They underline, exercise, and play upon your weaknesses, not your strengths.

Surrounding yourself with negative or alien standards of judgment can be draining and confusing. It's like being in a foreign country or in the wrong clothes. You eventually lose your bearings. This is what happens to a lot of people when they arrive in L.A. or New York. They no longer feel like they can still apply their own standards of good and bad taste, morality, or aesthetics. They forget who they are. Friends won't let you do that.

A person who inspires you doesn't have to be a friend you see regularly. He or she can be at the reach of e-mail or the phone. The feeling of connection and relief you've experienced in front of a certain painting suggests that your circle of friends can also include people you've never met.

▶▶70. AVOID YOUR ENEMIES COMPLETELY.

"No one can make you feel inferior without your consent."— Eleanor Roosevelt

Your enemies aren't right, but you believe they are. You give them whatever power they have over you. The doubt you think they feel about you is actually the one you feel in yourself. The net they supposedly have to trip you with is the one you put up yourself. We give our enemies arms to turn on ourselves.

We create our enemies, maybe, to push an internal struggle into physical, manifest form. There's no excuse and no need for anyone to take, or for you to give up, what's yours, especially when it's your confidence, your plans, your hopes or dreams.

If thinking about someone else and what they might think overwhelms rather than spurs your work, forget about it. Because your enemies' power stems from your own self-doubt, you have the power to escort them out of your life. Or at least to avoid them.

The world is big enough for you and all your enemies, along with your friends, to succeed. No one should need to triumph over anyone to get what they need. What you need is not in anyone else but in your own work. Get on with it and let them do the same.

▶▶ 71. BUDGET YOUR EMOTIONAL SUPPORT.

Around production, you'll draw beyond your usual limits of emotional support. Cast and crew will take all you have to give. And that's before your work (which is where it belongs) takes what's left.

Be aware of your own limits. Giving more than you can, all the time, is the emotional equivalent of expecting yourself to bench-press sets of a VW bug, instead of proverbially lifting it off your child with the unique adrenaline provided by a real emergency. People don't know what your emotional limits are unless you tell them. If you don't know yourself, this will be hard to do. Giving more than you can doesn't necessarily do a service to your friendship with the person who is asking, because you will resent them later.

Just as you have only so much money in the bank, you have only so much emotional support available from yourself, friends, and family. Spend it wisely. While it is a renewable resource, it takes some time to put back.

Are you counting on a boy/girlfriend, wife or husband, for your anticipated neediness during production? This can be dangerous. Since you're likely to expect more from them, you're likely to be more disappointed.

Ask yourself:

• Is this relationship stable?
• Does he or she require more from you than you're used to taking from him or her?
• Is a power shift possible?
• Is she or he capable of the shift? Or will it backlash, with your partner reverting to more childish and desperate neediness?
• Are you jealous? Are they? Do either of you feel the need to keep an eye on each other?
• Will the pressure of production only make things worse?
• Do you have good examples of dealing with stress in your relationship in your shared past that you can start talking about right now?

Don't wait for production to test your support partners. In fact, don't test them at all. Testing a loved one's loyalty backfires. By definition, a test is something that someone can fail. People will, and people do. Especially when they know they're being tested. Tests mean that trust has already been suspended. In other words, that you've already failed the friendship.

Rather than passing out tests, plan ahead. Be a careful, sensitive, honest judge of what people can give, and let them give it. Be honest about what you already know ahead of time, and adjust accordingly, planning for other sources of support.

If in your heart you think you're going to break up with a romantic partner, consider the following, and consider being selfish.

If it's the kind of relationship where you get lots of support but you don't think it has a long-term future, stay. And thank the person, every day, for the support they give. Feeling guilty? Tell the person, if you haven't already, that you don't think this will work out for the future. If they're healthy, they may leave. But then again, often there's something in it for them to stay. They may not be ready to leave, either. Carson McCullers wrote that in a couple, there's someone who loves and someone who lets themselves be loved. Your partner may need you to play the latter role. During production, you may play it better than ever.

If it's the kind of relationship where you're giving all the support and you've been wanting and needing to leave, leave. Especially if you know things are just going to get worse during production, because you'll be spending that much more time away. You don't want to come home at three A.M. from a shoot and be yelled at or face a pouting partner. The neediest people only become needier under stress. They will pull out all the emotional blackmail they can get their hands on, and only make things worse for you.

As fraught as emotional support can be from people you love, remember that it's still better to get it from off the set. Directors who forget this (as in, "You've got to work on my film or I'll die. I need you to save my life!") are hard to take.

▶▶ 72. JEALOUSY HAPPENS. WATCH FOR IT. THEN IGNORE IT COMPLETELY.

The green-eyed beast has a number of heads, equally ugly, that you may be familiar with:

1. **The "your friend made it and now you're jealous" sort**

   If you know what this feels like, take a moment to think about what that means about you. In short, low self-esteem. You have a limited sense of your, and the world's, possibilities and are operating under the false idea that life is a zero-sum game. Jealousy has no productive value, so consider this:

   Your friend's success just boosted your own chances. She has just raised the water level for both of you. If your friend goes off and gets her film set up at a major studio and receives a big payday, then she'll have a lot more clout than when she was a temp at Pizza Hut. You now know one more person with some level of power than you knew before. You are both more influential. You can share information. She can show you the way. You have to stay friends with this person, of course, for that to happen.

   It's no fun having a jealous friend; it's like not having a friend at all. Jealousy smells through your clothes, so try, as best you can, not to have it. If you can't overcome it, don't try to hide it with sweet perfumes. Just tell your friend. And laugh about it together, until it sheds.

2. **The "your friend has made it and now she's embarrassed and all weird" problem**

   Among the quirky reactions to sudden success: embarrassment. The one who got the break feels happy but a bit embarrassed next to friends who are still at Pizza Hut, waiting for theirs. If the embarrassment gets the best of successful people, they can distance themselves from old friends because they don't want to risk inadvertently rubbing people's noses in their success. They fear people's jealousy and being made to feel guilty. They fear losing the next round of success and having the same people laugh at them.

Be patient. Continue to act normal even if they don't. They'll eventually need to come back to their real friends. If you remain an even-keeled reminder of that friendship, they'll find their way back to themselves, and to you, faster.

3. The "your friends are jealous of you" problem

This is a drag. People who are jealous of you feel, or fear, that you're in their way. This is, of course, a fantasy—merely a concrete way to tell the story of their (at least, current) failure. Rather than getting on with their work, their jealousy casts you as a villain, either representative of, or truly directly to blame for, the problems in their lives. They funnel their fears of the unknown into a drama in which you're supposed to play the bad guy. The fantasy protects them from doing their own work and living their own life. One way they may "cope" is by attacking you or gossiping to others. Don't even bother to respond. The drama they're setting up serves their need for continued antagonism, which allows them to continue to shirk courage and responsibility.

One more thing: jealousy is a taboo emotion. People find it more difficult to own up to than anger or love. For good reason: it has no justification. For this reason you're going to need to trust your instincts when it comes to sensing jealousy in others. Not to make you paranoid, but if you feel someone's jealous, that's probably the best sign that they are. What to do next? Ignore it, and ignore them. Or, if you care about the relationship, tell them you think they're jealous. They might agree, with the relief a thief has of being caught, unburdened from carrying such an ugly and self-destructive secret.

▶▶ 73. THOSE THAT CAN TEACH . . .

To the idea that "when the student is ready, the teacher will come," we add a bit of a footnote: Do your homework and carefully evaluate teachers before you commit.

The basics you need in any teacher-student relationship follow. How many of the following questions can you answer with a definitive yes?

A. Will you hit it off?

Does he or she . . .

1. Come to class on time?

2. Have a syllabus? Plan ahead?

3. Turn off their beeper in class?

4. Use up the full class time, even the first day, because there is a lot to teach and every moment counts?

5. Acknowledge you outside of class?

6. Keep a TA for long?

7. Not treat you differently because of something inherent about you (gender, skin color, language of origin, sexuality, religion, etc.), but believe you when you say there is a difference to your experience?

8. Ask you questions? Ask for your opinion?

9. Say, "I don't know" when they don't?

10. Say, "That's a good question" and mean it?

11. Take you seriously when you say that you need financial aid, and help you (a) find less expensive ways to get through potentially expensive assignments, and/or (b) help you sort out the red tape of the school's loans and grants applications?

12. Accept coffee invitations to talk more?

13. Let you read last semester's student evaluations of their class?

14. Have peace with their relationship to the industry?

B. Will there be bumps in the road?

Some causes or signs of distress in teacher-student relationships follow. Which can you answer with no?

Does he or she . . .

1. Lose control of the class to someone else's agenda?

2. Make reference to going out and getting drunk with students?

3. Worse, raise an eyebrow to indicate what happened while getting drunk?

4. Use only their own films as examples?

5. Never use their own work for examples?

6. Have an unreasonable fear of technology, manifest even through operating the basics: the projector, the VCR, e-mail?

7. Need to tell you that video—and now digital video—is a passing thing?

8. Maintain utter cluelessness toward the school's rules? Or arrogantly dismiss the bureaucratic hurdles you have to deal with?

9. Subtly compete with you and/or other talented students in class?

C. Bonus round: Will they stick around for the long haul? (That is: Do they have mentor potential?)

Are they . . .

1. Still in awe of the medium?

2. Happy for students who've had careers?

3. Confident that you can always do something new?

4. Genuinely happy to be teaching?

5. Able to see and appreciate what's unique about you?

6. Able to see a positive future for you? Not worried about how long it will take for you to get there?

7. Mature enough to recognize that some of your issues, or limitations, are simply a matter of your age?

8. Engaged by joy, ideas, and potential?

Not all teachers have the capacity or willingness to be mentors. Or they have it, but they're not the right teacher for you at the time. Worse than not having a mentor is investing the power in the wrong person. Remember that a mentor, or inspirational teacher or role model, does not have to be from the world of film. Director and NYU film school graduate Susan Seidelman credits as her mentor the English teacher who introduced her to Virginia Woolf.

NYU Film Industry Liaison Jeremiah Newton, who runs one of the oldest film mentorship programs in the country, counsels graduate students to seek mentors who are actively working as industry professionals, yet ready to listen to (and, by implication, learn from) their mentees. Critical to a productive relationship, Jeremiah says, is for mentees to have something tangible, such as a script or film in progress, for mentors to respond to. The relationship should be collaborative. It gives neither party enough back if it's only about worshiping the mentor or the films they have worked on.

▸▸ 74. IF THEY DON'T BELIEVE IN YOU, THEY MIGHT NOT BELIEVE IN ANYONE.

Faith is a gift. Some people have it, like a genetic talent. The ones who really don't have it may not be able to believe in you or anyone, including themselves.

If you want to make a film, you have the entrepreneur gene— either latent or already evident. It's a rare kind of faith, and it puts you in the same boat with people launching their own start-ups, with little more than an idea and a reserve of confidence.

They, like you, have to manage the multiple and never-ending tasks of budgeting, rebudgeting, financing, refinancing, marketing, sales, planning, hiring, managing, firing. Make a film and you'll appreciate the struggles of the entrepreneur, and admire the success of anyone with the focus, dedication, and smarts to make their new business a success. You'll admire them because you'll recognize the same guts film requires from you. Business is, of course, creative. Especially when you define creativity as problem solving, which it is. Business people have to deal with the stress of the constantly shifting ground of the marketplace and the pressure of its one standard: the bottom line.

Conversely, captains of industry, including nascent ones, will recognize and appreciate the same in you. They can relate to your need to take calculated risks, and your single-mindedness for turning the leap of faith into a product: a film. They'll respect the fact that you're your own boss, and that you're not coasting by on a paycheck someone else signs every month. Learn from, and draw support from, successes in any field of business. Graze through the business books section and pick up business magazines and read about people like you. Invite someone you admire to lunch. They're likely to admire you right back.

▶▶75. TEN ANSWERS TO "ARE YOU DONE YET?"

People may not have the most charitable, constructive motives for asking if you're "done." To these you can give short answers:

1. No.

3. And you?

3. Why do you ask?

4. The last time I remember you were . . . (let them fill it in).

If, on the other hand, your questioner seems to have a more empathic appreciation of the long road involved in writing and financing a film, your answers can reflect more of the real truth: that writing and selling are a process, and you encountered unexpected challenges along the way. As in:

5. The more I work on it, the more I realize what it's really about.

6. Yes. I'm done with the version I had told you about. But it's going to have to go in a different direction for me to stay involved.

7. No. And I wish it was. But I'm going to stick with it. The darkest moment is just before dawn. It's harder than I thought. But maybe it's because I've discovered how meaningful it is to me.

8. I'm rewriting it for:

   • an actor I'm friends with
   • an executive who's interested
   • a different rating
   • different financing
   • a new budget

- different locations
- different collaborators who have their own input
- my lawyer, who anticipated some legal problems
- a different age group
- a younger audience
- a more mass audience
- a different take on the violence

9. My writing partner and I have been working on different projects. It's been hard to get the time to work on this together.

10. My goals for it have changed. I wrote it for sale, and now I want to make it myself (or vice versa).

Maybe none of these responses are true. But they can be better than no answer at all.

12

IT'S A SAD DOG WHO CAN'T WAG ITS OWN TAIL

▸▸76. FAKING CONFIDENCE.

Listen closely and you can often hear disjuncture between what people say and what they actually mean. This is called subtext, and almost every line in real life has one. It's re-creating this very tension in your scripts and getting it reflected in your actors' performances that will make your films lifelike. Awareness of how you express this tension in your real life can help you manage it when you really need to.

Like, say, when you walk into a film executive's office to pitch your script. You already know that instead of thinking, "I am a lowly insect, full of doubt, and I am so desperate I would lick your boots," you really should try to give yourself a more positive internal monologue. Self-actualization gurus sell these at a dime a dozen, but you don't believe them enough to make them work. It's no wonder. Lines like "I'm achieving my full potential right now, and always," or "I'm so fabulous I scare myself," or "I am a self-actualizing machine, and I cannot be stopped. Feel the glare of my capped teeth," are all about convincing yourself that you are something or someone you know you're not (and wouldn't want to be).

Rather than give yourself an inner mantra in which you pretend to be something you're not, it's much more effective to think about an action with which you're very familiar. Say someone's knocked on your door and you go to answer it. If it's someone you want to see, your next action will be to welcome them into your house. Everything you say and do while they're visiting will be motivated by the desire to make them feel comfortable. The underlying action behind your speech will be "to welcome them to my house," and it will work. A nice side effect of this message is that by helping your guest feel comfortable, you will naturally feel and appear confident.

Use the same motivation even when you're not welcoming someone to your house. Indeed, try it when you go into that meeting with the executive. As you walk through the door, think to yourself that the purpose of the meeting is "to welcome him to my house." Like a good "host," you will naturally take the attention off yourself and make yourself feel like the one in control. By thinking principally in terms of helping him feel comfortable, you will forget about your own discomfort. You will project an impression of generosity rather than one of neediness.

Speech that is backed up with the motivation "to welcome you to my house" sounds much better than speech laced with the question "Is it OK if I sit here?" Here are some other internal motivations to keep in mind when in unfamiliar situations:

- To help you relax
- To start the party
- To share the joke
- To let you in on a secret
- To share the joy
- To give you a gift. To watch you open it.

Notice that each of these statements implies what you have to give rather than what you're there to ask for. They allow you to hold on to your own power rather than give it away at the first handshake.

The next tricks are even simpler, and should let your self-confidence grow faster than sea monkeys:

1. **As you walk onto the set, think to yourself:** "Everybody's nervous. It's my job to help them not to be."

2. **Take baby steps.** Understand that film offers the false promise of mastery. Film is an art, and by definition, you can never learn everything. Don't expect to. Kids build their self-confidence by mastering a series of small skills. Tying their shoes. Zipping their windbreakers. Once they've learned how to perform these finite actions, they rightfully know there's nothing more they'll ever need to learn about them. This in itself gives them confidence. Enough to fuel the next step in their learning. No one expects you to pull off an Ozu-level masterwork when you've never picked up a camera.

3. **Give Steven Seagal or your little brother some career advice.** Figure out what they should do next and what they shouldn't do. Notice how clear and obvious it all is, and what an expert you are. Now take your own advice.

4. **Don't forget the basics.** Use a firm handshake. If you don't have something positive to say, don't say anything at all. Don't wear anything that makes you feel uncomfortable. Leave plenty of travel time.

5. **Adopt the "Don't complain, don't explain" ethic.** If you're late, don't complain about the traffic. It's not the traffic's fault that you're late. It's yours. Apologize quickly and move on. Don't come to the meeting needing anything (a glass of water, the bathroom). You sabotage your strength immediately and give away the upper hand. Don't give your power away for something so trivial.

6. **Rehearse the putt mentally.** Athletes and surgeons rehearse their moves mentally so that when they show up to do it for real, it's as if for the second or two thousandth time. You can never rehearse your pitch too many times, in your mind's eye as well as in full voice.

▸▸77. PITCHING IS STORYTELLING BY ANOTHER NAME.

Pitching is telling a great campfire story to grown-ups. You're sure that because sales is involved, it's something wildly more complicated and unnatural.

But storytelling *is* selling by its nature. If sales is the transfer of belief from one person to another, the same goes for a story. To tell a story effectively you need to "sell" it—transferring your interest in it to someone else.

You entertain by making your audience get pulled in by the lure of the story. So that they're involved in it and nothing else. Going into a pitch meeting does not have to feel like more of a sales job than going in to tell a great story.

Stories are seduction. They desire, and require, the audience's attention. A branch of literary theory has said that stories literally don't exist until they are received, enacted, and embodied by an audience. Stories need to hook an audience and weave them into their very existence in order even to exist.

Here are some ways to make the most of your partnership with your audience:

1. The most important thing is passion. Joy is good. Some people think joy is corny. It's not. Being joyful doesn't make you stupid. It implies self-esteem.

2. Clarity is almost as important as joy. Know your story. Not just the linear facts of it, but the very conflict that will give the audience a reason to watch.

3. Know the point to the story. This is something like the theme and something like the moral. But basically it's what you want to give them. What you want them to think about at the end.

4. Know the way the story ends. Stories exist for their endings. Every scene in your film should move us to this climactic moment.

5. Let the audience know what's at stake from the outset. This will let them understand the tone of the story and react accordingly. They won't laugh when they're not supposed to.

6. Gauge your audience. Reflect the audience's desires through your storytelling. Make adjustments as you go along. Like a lover, frankly. Faster, slower, more or less lingering. Then, when you've totally synchronized your rhythm, go go go, unstoppably to the end.

7. You're talking about a film, and even if you weren't, it's a good idea to put them in front of images. They should always know where they are, by way of getting engaged.

8. True conflict is a choice between two bad choices. Set that up and an audience will stop watching and start engaging themselves, as if the conflict was theirs.

9. If they give you an idea, work it in and let the story follow their momentum as much as possible. Chances are, you won't be starting your pitch at the top of the studio's hierarchy. You depend on this junior executive to feel the story is her own enough to want to sell it to her boss.

10. Practice. If you don't feel like doing it, it's because you need to.

11. Establish eye contact meaningfully from the very outset and hold on to it throughout the pitch, shifting your gaze only to take in the other people in the room, one at a time.

12. Remember that film, taken as a commercial product, is merely a means to an end: a tool to capture a paying audi-

ence. What you're really selling is the audience who will pay to see the movie, and yourself and the film as the Pied Piper who can deliver it.

13. Don't talk a blue streak. Let them ask questions. It's not for you to overexplain why exactly the story moves from point A to point Z. Instead, you should take them from A to M, and then from R to Z. Quickly. Writers tend to be insecure if it's not the written matter that's being considered, says screenwriter Amy Dawes. They basically want to read the whole script to the person on the other side of the table. Know your story well enough to know what to leave out.

How else to prepare? Remember that people will invest only in the things they are sure will get made. You want to make it clear that the product you are proposing has all of the elements in place except the ones they can offer you. Communicate that you can get these elsewhere if not from them.

Regardless of the questions they ask, these are always the wrong answers:

1. I don't own the rights, but I'm sure that once they hear about this idea and with your support we can get them easily. You have lawyers who do that, right?

2. I fired the cowriter. But that's OK because it was my idea anyway and I didn't have a contract with him, so it's cool. (No, it's not.)

3. I have no idea how much this will cost to make.

4. That's hard to explain.

5. Let me think about that . . . I'll get back to you.

6. I don't know.

7. I don't have any actors in mind.

8. I don't know who the audience for this would be. Every-one?

9. I don't have any leads on financing other than you.

13

GETTING THROUGH THE MOST TERRIBLE, WONDERFUL FEW WEEKS OF YOUR LIFE SO FAR

▶▶78. DELEGATE.

In the category of insanely simple, deeply valuable, and compulsively ignored advice, along with "wear sunscreen" and "write thank-you notes," is "delegate."

Mort Zarcoff, the icon of the USC old school—the man who oversaw the advanced production class from the mod era of sideburns through their second coming—had this wise word to pass on: delegate. He intoned it gravely to Camille before she started preproduction on her advanced project. She nodded, then failed to follow his advice.

It came back to her only when she fell on her face in the middle of the street in the midst of the first day of shooting. She was running back from the supermarket, where she had bought decaf tea bags for the actors. She was not only directing the movie, she was also in it. In the next scene, even. Her costume, which she was wearing, could have ripped. Or, even more inconveniently, she could have been hit by a car. In short, she shouldn't have been running to or from the market.

Delegate is another word for trust. If you can't trust other people with responsibility and the power to make decisions, you'll be making the film by yourself, which you can't do. You're as strong as your capacity to trust, paired with your talent for trusting the right people.

People think of directing films as a chance to have control. People are wrong. Directing is a humbling experience in which you realize that you have absolute control over absolutely nothing. If you're still clinging to the fantasy of control, be warned that you'll eventually be forced to give it up. Whether it's to the elements, the circumstances of minor and major disasters, or to the fact that no one can find the key to your location.

Better to give your so-called control away to people who can bring it back to you in the form of choices. Give the production designer the power to go without you to select the props, but request he bring back some choices. When he comes back, you'll get to choose from a number of options. You don't give away your power by sharing it, you multiply it.

More choice is more power and more control. Your power becomes manifest when you share it—the more you share it through judicious delegating, the more you have.

▶▶ 79. NOW DELEGATE SMART.

Even with a fully staffed crew, there are jobs that fall outside the definitions, yet are nevertheless critical to the life of your shoot. These can be as large or as small as stalling an angry landlord who claims you're trespassing, entertaining investors when they drop by, or clearing the air in a dark moment on the set with a joke.

These are not jobs you can put a title on, and they're not the kind of things you can do all on your own for very long. These small, unpredictable annoyances are the straws that would break your back.

The most effective delegating comes from asking people to do things that come naturally to them. Prepare help in advance by imagining who among your cast and crew is gifted at handling the small stuff without a sweat.

Imagine you're giving a dinner party for all of your crew, friends, family, and romantic entanglements. First question: Who stays to clean up? You're actually lucky if there's anyone. This is someone who loves you in such a way that they'll put aside their desire to go home long enough to help you get to bed at a reasonable time. This is someone who actually cares about your health.

If they're a friend from the real world outside your production, you may ask them if they would do you the honor and favor of being your official "emergency blanket"—the person you can call no matter what the time of need. If they're actually on your crew, you may want them to assume the role of assistant director (A.D.) or line producer, the people who are responsible for running your set, with, ideally, a proper mix of your ambitions and health in mind.

Now go back to your imaginary dinner party and ask yourself: Who are the friends and crew members who will find something to talk about with any of the other guests? Who can you count on to check on the lasagna? To keep an eye on the children? To answer the door or the phone? To vamp for you while you finish cooking, or dressing, or both? To calm someone down who's been drinking too much? To turn an awkward moment into a funny joke? To listen to someone who's gotten upset without embarrassing them further?

At the very least, the dinner party test should help you recognize who on your crew is not oriented toward performing these tasks, so that you don't delegate the wrong role to the wrong person.

Now, if you haven't already done so, identify which role you take most naturally. When you return the favor to a friend who helped on your shoot (and you should), put your particular talent to work. It doesn't have to mean helping on a film, especially if your friend comes from the "real world." Maybe you can pay them back by staying to do the dishes.

▶▶80. LONG AFTER YOU WATCH YOUR FILM, YOU'LL PLAY THE EXPERIENCE BACK IN YOUR MIND. KEEP IT PG.

Once it's all done, you'll actually watch your film only a few times. But long after anyone sees or remembers the film, you'll remember the experience of making it, which is why you want to make it a good one. That argument you're tempted to have could play forever in syndication in the theater of your mind, so hold your tongue.

When you watch your film, you won't see what other people see. You'll see a heat-sensitive rendering of your pain and/or joys in making the film. Of course you'll see the mistakes—the boom shadow, the missing shot, the dull light. But worse, you'll see, and relive, the reasons why they happened. How you had to argue with the actor to get even a slice of a performance, how you broke up with your boyfriend after that day's shooting, how the scene could have been cut so much better if you and the editor hadn't had that fight two days before picture lock.

The laser disk track of reminiscence plays for you at every screening of your film and in your mind spontaneously, even when you didn't turn it on. Make a real effort at directing this one. Avoid a nightmare loop of mean talk and stab wounds, playing over and over again without forgiveness. Try instead to prepare a future memory of a caring, effective work environment, giving rise to miracles of synchronicity and amazing contributions made by each of the crew. *This* is the film you're making. Make it a film you want to watch again and again.

▶▶81. PREARRANGE AN ALL-HOURS CRISIS LINE.

A caveat to "don't ever let them see you sweat" is "make sure there's someone who does." Preferably someone who has nothing to do with the production. A friend or family member with unconditional love and two feet in the real world. Camille counted on her sister Florence, whose very voice was a trip back to the reality coat checkroom where she had left hers.

Someone who can say simple, true things like "That hurt" or "That was mean" can soothe you magically. Like your mother kissing a boo-boo to make it better, the very acknowledgment that something bad happened lets the healing begin.

Someone who knows you very well can invite the other element of a confession: helping you see where your faults lie. It's not good just to complain. If you don't know where you went wrong (and you did), it might happen again.

Your own sense of guilt will come through your voice even as you're complaining. Your little sister can hear it, just as she did when she knew she was going to get an apology out of you. The power you regain from understanding your responsibility in any skirmish will let you get your confidence back in time to walk onto the set tomorrow.

If need be, rehearse an apology to your cast/crew member with your sister. She'll help you get it right: not too broad so you seem like a wimp who's trying to be loved, or too narrow so that you seem petty. Walk in with the apology ready, make it, and move on through that day's work. Your sister will still be there at the other end of the phone at the end of it all. Still sure that you're full of faults. And just as sure that you're wonderful.

▶▶82. MAKE YOUR BED EVERY DAY AND KNOW IT'LL BE THERE FOR YOU TO COME BACK TO.

Marathon runners say a helpful strategy is to break a run into manageable chunks. After running seventy miles (!), even these supermarathoners say it can be hard to think in terms of the next thirty. Their advice is to think of five miles at a time instead. It constitutes to them a meaningful goal, because it's within their grasp.

Making your bed and thinking about how nice it will be to come home to helps you break your shoot down into more manageable pieces—namely, one day at a time. At some low point you'll see the image of your bed, clean and made, waiting for you. You'll understand that you're taking care of yourself and that, if nothing else, you can count on that. That's a good feeling. It's a simple mental strategy that works, especially when you consider the alternative: leave a mess and you have a mess to come home to.

▶▶ 83. KEEP YOUR FRIENDS SO YOU CAN LAUGH ABOUT IT ALL LATER.

Pain, mixed with a bit of distance, is the stuff of comedy. Still, you won't have anyone to laugh with if you cause pain to your friends.

Keep your friends through the thick and the thin, and you'll notice that it's possible to almost "enjoy" either the good or bad equally. In our friendship, sharing failure is as meaningful—and in some ways, as fun—as sharing success. Both make us laugh.

Because the friendship is more valuable to us than anything else we encounter along the way, the distinction between failure and success is not great. Both are simply experiences that we share together. It's the friendship that lasts, and the friendship that matters more to both of us.

▶▶ 84. RUN THE RACE TO FINISH AND YOU'LL HAVE WON.

You're not running against anyone else but yourself. Ultimately, no one cares how long it took you to finish your script, or produce, direct, and edit your movie if it's good and they can sell it. You can become an overnight success after ten years of trying to be. No one's holding a stopwatch to your time. They're too busy worrying about their own.

So run at your own pace. Don't set your expectations to someone else's unless it helps you finish your race. In racing, it's true that an external standard measures relative success: 2:36 minutes versus 3 hours. But we'd bet that if you finished a marathon in *any* number of hours, you'd feel a sense of accomplishment. Same with making your film.

Since this isn't a matter of 26.2 miles uphill, but of 26.2 days, months, or years, the challenge isn't on your leg muscles but on your heart and brain. Many are the excuses to give up, including giving in to someone else's standards of success.

Only you know what you're capable of. Only you know what

constitutes a stretch, and a success. Camille ran a minitriathlon. Ran isn't quite the word for it. Far and away the last person in the pack, on the last lap, she strained to push her bike up the hill and walk it down. Just as she was lamenting her miserable last-ness, a group of four women in a golf cart putted up the hill. "Are you in a race?" one of them asked. "Something like that," she answered. "Are you first?" one asked, noticing that there was nobody else in sight. "Not first. Last," Camille answered. But it didn't matter to the women. They congratulated her for being on her feet at all, and went on with their battery-powered tour.

14

THE ROAD TRIP TEST

▸▸ 85. WOULD YOU GO ON A THREE-WEEK (OR THREE-MONTH) ROAD TRIP WITH THIS (POTENTIAL CREW) PERSON?

Think of three friends you'd want to go on a road trip with.

Now picture the four of you in a Ford Pinto, without air conditioning, driving across the country with only dirty roadside bathroom breaks and an econopack of SlimJims to console you.

Still friends? Now add a few flat tires, getting lost in the wrong desert, and very dirty laundry.

Now imagine the same trip with your crew.

- Who's whining, "Are we there yet?"
- Who tells a good story? Who listens well?
- Who wants to hurry up and get home to start another job?
- Who always needs to eat? Who never wants to?
- Who shares the bill fairly?
- Who lingers at every other rest stop flirting with the cashier?
- Who would you trust to read a map? Who refuses to ask for directions?
- Who says, "I told you so" over a wrong turn?
- Who do you feel safe enough with so that you could sleep while they're driving?

The rarest of friends can survive traveling together, let alone making a film together. When you live on your own, you're barely aware of the thousands of choices you make during a day over basic things—like when to eat and when to sleep. When you travel with someone else, you become keenly aware of these decisions, and who's been monopolizing them. Everything becomes an issue, because everything is.

Choose crew who you could have fun with on the hottest day in that Pinto. You'll end up as friends, and may possibly have a film to show for the trip.

▶▶ 86. BEWARE THE IDES OF MARCH.

Et tu, Bruté?

Julius Caesar's famous last words in Shakespeare's eponymous play are weighted with the irony that Caesar is more pained by his friend's betrayal than by the sword Brutus just stabbed in his back.

Betrayal hurts. By definition, betrayal is wrought by people we trust. There is no betrayal by enemies. They can be more predictable than friends.

We are not saying that your best friends will betray you *exactly*, although the toughest stories we know from film school and its aftermath are about this. Here are a few in brief, without betraying any names:

- A producer who spent over half of an ultra-low budget film's funds on an enormous, catered gourmet meal featuring striped sea bass and deviled eggs, then skipped town.
- A vengeful production designer who sold the production's props in an impromptu yard sale.
- An A.D. who told the film school faculty the production was wildly behind schedule in the hopes of killing the production so he could spend more time with his girlfriend.
- An editor and producer who planned a coup against the director and succeeded.
- Another editor and another producer who planned a coup against a director and succeeded, only to do the same thing to each other one week later.

- A producer who hired herself to replace a director supposedly with his permission and yet completely without his knowledge—as he was out of town.
- A producing team of best friends who sued each other—after they "made it" (this has happened to multiple friends).
- An editor who coordinated secret production meetings without the director to convince the crew to mutiny and work on a film he wanted to direct.

All of the above individuals were friends with each other, sometimes best friends. We use the past tense for a reason.

There really is no way to defend yourself in advance for this kind of thing. To protect yourself from your friends is the route to paranoia, loneliness, and misery. You can't prepare for war, says Camille's father, George, who survived World War II's Siberian work camps. The best you can do is strengthen yourself in peacetime so that your spirit and clarity survive war time. You can't prepare yourself for what people might do under stress, but you should be ready to recognize the behavior if it happens, and not make any excuses for it.

Don't lose your standards, don't compromise your barometer of what's OK, don't lose your instinctive sense of what's right and wrong—or you've lost yourself, and the war—by which we mean your film.

▸▸ 87. LOYALTY OVER EXPERIENCE ANYDAY.

When the ingredient of loyalty is absent on a film set, the difficult becomes impossible. Without loyalty a crew or cast can be less than eager to help you triumph over your mistakes.

Some years ago, Tiare was hired on an art department job for a commercial, shooting at a racetrack in the middle of the California nowhere. The production designer had inspired her loyalty by hiring her a number of times and by always saying thank you. So when he called and asked if she would drive out to the desert and work on this commercial at a moment's notice, she said, "Sure." At the end of a long day that began with a four-hour drive to get to the location, the client said—without any prior discussion—that they wanted the walls of the racetrack a different color. It was eight o'clock and it needed to be that way by dawn the next day.

The production designer, backed into a corner, imprudently said yes, his crew could do it. The crew now faced covering an entire racetrack, the length of at least a football field, with colored cardboard since the location would not let them paint it. The "crew" was two people: Tiare and someone she had just met.

Imagine two want ads for that job:

1. Wanted: someone great at stapling cardboard, or
2. Wanted: someone who will stay up all night because of loyalty or work ethic or both

It would have been much easier, so much easier, to just say, "No, it's not possible to do this overnight. You couldn't pay me enough!" But since the production designer had earned their loyalty and best effort, even in the face of a moment of poor judgment, they got the job done.

And redone, because after the first all-nighter of putting up cardboard, the early morning dew rippled the surface of the board and they had to do it again—on one hour's sleep between them. Then in the middle of shooting, the wind created by the cars speeding around the track pulled the boards down in a terrifying domino effect that brought all the race cars to a screeching, rubber-burning halt. They had to put the boards up again, this time using bigger staples.

Sometime during that fifty-six-hour marathon they became friends, and they've stayed (loyal) friends through this and many other films. And, oh yes, the production designer never forgot the favor, and neither did the client, who was so impressed by their persistence that they explicitly requested the same art department crew for their next commercial. It certainly wasn't their cardboard-stapling skills that earned them that request—it was their willingness to go all the way.

The big open secret about filmmaking is that, with a couple of exceptions, very few jobs on a film set require deep or significant experience. The logic, after all, to film school is that students learn how to make films in a series of on-the-job exercises. After a couple of crewing experiences, people know their way around making a film with at least a basic degree of competence. (The only true exception we can think of is stunt coordinating. For obvious reasons you want someone with real experience to do that job, or cut the stunts out altogether.)

Loyalty, on the other hand, is a quality that may not be learned in the same way. To find a loyal cast for low-budget films, Steven Rodriguez, Los Angeles City College film student, asks actors and crew to come back *repeatedly* for auditions and meetings before he gives them the job. He does this because he needs to know that the person is willing to take action for the film now, without even knowing if they have the job yet and knowing full well, on top of that, that they will not make much or any money working for him even if they do get the job. The logic for Steve is, if someone is willing to happily keep showing up on time for any meeting you set, chances are that you have someone who will really work hard for you under any conditions. That's loyalty.

▶▶ 88. BEWARE OF TWO-FOR-ONE AND BOTH-OR-NONE DEALS.

If they come together, they'll leave together. Crew or cast members who package themselves as a two-for-one deal hold their first loyalty to each other, not to the project. If one of them becomes unhappy, then the other one will probably become unhappy, too. If one wants to leave the shoot, then the other one will, too. As a result of coming into the shoot as a package, each has the voting power and unwarranted influence of two people.

On a set, the only thing worse than a couple of friends or lovers loyal only to each other is when they break up. The crew is then compelled to break up into a psychotic war over whose side they take, the intrigues of which have nothing to do with which shot is next.

We're not saying you shouldn't hire people who like each other. Just don't hire people who will work only if they can bring along their friend and protective shogun. Two is enough to talk behind anyone's back. Enough to share a maddening joke they won't let anyone in on. It's enough to keep a secret, and enough to start a mutiny.

On one particularly ill-fated first-year film project at AFI, the producer-initiator hired a director who said he wouldn't do the project unless he could bring along a certain cinematographer. Since the D.P. was very talented, the producer considered himself fortunate and said yes. All went smoothly until the producer and the director began to have conflicts over how the story should be told and the director quit and took the cinematographer with him.

Although the cinematographer and the producer had no beef with each other vis-à-vis the story, the D.P. told the producer he had no choice but to leave when the director did. His first loyalty was to the director, not to the project or the producer. Staying on after the director left over creative differences would be taken as a breach of loyalty.

Unfortunately, the director and D.P.'s leaving resulted in the editor and his assistant's (another two-for-one deal) jumping ship, too, because they felt that there was no way the film could recover from such a loss so late in the process. The editor and his friend joined a project that was already shot but had just lost an editor.

The producer was now left to recrew not just one but *four* positions before the film could start shooting. Losing more than one key crew member in the eleventh hour of preproduction (and worse, during your shoot) can create a domino effect of doom and instability in your remaining crew. Everyone gets worried that they may be on a train that is no longer moving and may want to get off fast so as not to miss more viable opportunities.

The strategic importance of avoiding two-for-one deals is greater than the risk of losing the two deal members for another reason: if it is a department head that quits, then the chances are greater you'll lose the whole department if the mutinying boss can offer them another gig soon.

There is little you can do to control this. Once you've hired a department head, you must give that person latitude to hire the people they see fit to staff their department. You don't want to hire every set dresser and camera loader unless you have to. You *want* to hire department heads who have a crew of people they work with regularly and can rely on. It means they are able to inspire a certain degree of loyalty from their team members, and are good to work for.

Our best advice: strive, as the director or producer, to be the common ground between your key crew members. If you and the project are what they all have in common, then the lines of loyalty are set in a way that will work for you in times of crisis, not against you.

▸▸89. IF YOU HAVE TO TALK ANYONE INTO WORKING ON THE FILM, DON'T.

Begging gives away your power, your self-worth, and the worth of your project. Since chances are you're not paying your cast and crew very much (or at all), these are the only values you have to offer. You need to protect them.

Someone who needs to be begged to do something and then accepts is in it for the flattery. They need to be needed. You'll never be able to give them enough. What you give will only prompt them to beg, in their silent way, for more. Once you beg someone to work on your film, you'll be begging them to stay through the whole shoot. If they never made the decision for themselves, they won't ever take the responsibility that goes with it.

Instead, the day will come, sooner rather than later, where they'll hold it against you. They'll harbor fantasies about the opportunities they missed. Even if it's just the chance to stay at home in a warm bed.

Or, they'll resent you for "making them" do something they're not particularly good at. The crew or cast member who is talked into working on your film, despite protestations, can hold you hostage later with the claim, "I never said I could do this. I only said I would." This logic takes the pressure off them to do anything well. If they fail, it's your fault for having told them they could do it, and for hiring them.

Beware if *you're* this type of person. If you find yourself working on projects or with people you don't truly admire, chances are, you're doing it because you need to be needed. You may enjoy situations that require the people who have hired you to constantly check in to make sure you are going to stay, to pump you up with praise and gratefulness. If this sounds like you, then be all the more sure that you do not seek to replicate this pattern in your own hiring process just because it is familiar to you. The begging tactics that worked on you may not be what you want to use when you cast your own film. That is, unless you are prepared to have those you hire use the same defenses you did, and for you to have to play the role of eternal coddler until the wrap.

The tone and the terms of your initial meeting set the dynamic of your work together. It's said of couples that the seeds to the breakup are planted in the first meeting. Usually, whoever starts with the power in the relationship keeps it. So don't start by begging and be left with the short end of a film when you could have had more.

▶▶ 90. DON'T BELIEVE THE HYPE. BELIEVE THE WORK.

Hype exists to sell something—sight (and sound) unseen. It's used to sell movies, since movies are among the rare commodities sold before the ultimate buying audience has a chance to see them. Hype, however, has no place in selling you on a crew member. You should watch their reel of work carefully, check references (more on this later), and meet, as extensively as necessary, in person.

A serious round of interviews with a slate of candidates for each position serves a number of purposes:

- **It creates an even playing field.** If you're at school and crewing from among friends and classmates, emotion can fog your decisions. A regular, levelheaded interview process in which you treat everyone the same, watch everyone's reel, etc., lends a dignity and structure to a process that should *not* be about favors. If you give anyone on your crew special treatment— from the way you hire them (without an interview) to the way you treat them on the set—everyone notices, and you've started to divide your crew into camps before production has even started.

- **It lets them know you're not desperate.** As we've said, as with romantic relationships, the tone you set from the beginning marks your dynamic from then on. They won't respect you if you're (too) easy. Make them work for your respect and attention and everyone wins, because they'll respect you, and when they do "win," they'll feel they've scored something of value.

- **It allows you to have a common set of expectations.** Without a common reference point established through viewing the work of your potential crew member, you have nothing with which to compare their performance on the set. If their hiring depended only on hype, they don't have a real standard to shoot for, and you don't have any reference points of their previous work to use as guidelines. When their work shows signs of weakness, in order to protect their reputation, they'll blame you, and this particular shoot, for it.

  If you hire someone based on nothing but glitter, that's all you have to fall back on. If, on the other hand, you hire someone based on your mutual respect for each other's work, you have from that point forward a shared vocabulary and set of expectations.

- **You can find out if they really did the work.** Talking with them about what's on the reel can reveal who was responsible for the way things came out. This can also serve to their advantage: they can explain problems in the footage that they truly had nothing to do with. You can learn a lot this way about the respect they have for other people's work. It's easy to point out other people's work when it's flawed; it takes maturity to appreciate and acknowledge when other people's work is good.

- **You can learn to what extent they take responsibility for their mistakes.** You're looking for the ones who do. These people are the true leaders, with the most authentic self-esteem. Paying attention to what went wrong means that they expected to find themselves in a leadership role again, and didn't want to repeat these mistakes again. You're going to be learning through this, too. You want to gauge their comfort, both with supporting your learning and accepting their own vulnerability and growth.

▸▸91. IF YOU CAN'T TALK DURING THE INTERVIEW, IT'LL ONLY GET WORSE.

Think of a favorite funny story. Think about telling it to your mother, versus your best friend, versus your great-aunt Sally, versus a police officer, versus the queen of England.

The story is funnier with some people than with others.

The story's essentials don't change, but the way you tell it does. You shape stories—indeed, all speech—to meet your audience. We don't ever speak in a vacuum. Try telling a story to the blank air. In order to do it, you need to imagine someone there to receive it. When we speak, we always speak to someone in particular. It's impossible to leave a message on an answering machine, for example, without imagining the person you're leaving it for. It's audience, or imagined audience, that gives us the words to use.

Your confidence—the ease with which you tell a story—is based not only on your level of comfort with your particular audience, but with your anticipation of how comfortable with and accepting they are of you. The easiest kind of talking is with friends. Not only because they can understand what you say, but because you *know* they can. Talking to them is like walking through an open door.

The opposite can be true, too. It's hard to talk to people who don't seem to already understand you. How you sound can depend on how receptive your cast and crew are to what you have to say. Therefore, the most important thing to listen for when interviewing a potential crew or cast member is how *you* sound. Are you funny telling a joke? It depends on whether you two naturally share a similar sense of humor. Are you nervous talking about something personal? You may rightly fear you're being judged or misunderstood. Hitting some silent pauses? You may not have anything you want to say to them, based on your (perhaps accurate) suspicion that there's nothing they want to hear.

Think about the Tower of Babel you're up against when it comes to communicating about your film. You're taking a kind of dream or ghost you have skimming through your brain, putting some one-dimensional approximation of it on paper, and then asking people to express it through camera angles, props, voice levels, etc. The process involves speaking a desperately shifting array of languages to try to explain the ephemeral. Language, from the get-go, is a compromise to the limitless, luminous film experience you hope to create. Your only chance is to start by sharing at least one language, with everyone on your cast and crew—and that begins with a conversation.

▶▶ 92. CHOOSE CREW WHO HAVE SOMETHING TO GAIN.

Money is not enough. Not that you have any. But even well-paying jobs need to offer more than money for employees to stay. These values include: challenge, prestige, fun, a chance to learn, a sense of meaning and purpose. The intangibles count. On your films they will count a lot.

When you've identified your crew positions, identify what you can legitimately offer in exchange for them. Then look for someone who wants what you can offer, and who can give something meaningful in return. Do not choose people who have everything to gain but nothing to give (i.e., losers). Don't put yourself in the position of having to convince them that what you have is what they need—even if it is (see "If you have to talk someone into working on the film, don't").

Be open to thinking about finding crew people outside the low-budget filmmaking community at large. For the producing position you can't offer pay or "profit participation" points if it's a short film that's never going to see any profit. What you can offer is exposure to every stage and cycle of production. This may be interesting to bored accountants or a business school student who wants to dip a toe into producing to see if they want to take the plunge. On their end of the deal, the fact that they don't have experience can be traded for their great organizational and people skills, understanding of financing models, work ethic, rich friends . . . the list goes on.

For the production design position, especially if you're not at a film school with a program in this, go looking at theater, arts, and architecture programs. Call the department, speak to a faculty member, and ask for student references. If they are students, they may even be able to get independent study or internship credit, which does carry a financial value. People who work in theater and architecture often spend a tremendous amount of time drudging through low-profile, low-concept tasks at their companies before they are given the opportunity to do something that is more creatively satisfying and conceptually "theirs." This makes them particularly susceptible to the lure of film work.

While the compensation you can offer—experience, learning, etc.—doesn't cost you money, it's not unlimited. You can give only so much mentoring and attention to so many people. As when you hire someone for money, you have to make sure that what you're giving is going to the right person.

▶▶ 93. TAKE REFERENCES VERY, VERY, VERY SERIOUSLY.

Ask for references and you're already ahead of the game. The problems begin when directors and producers face time crunches and decide references are a luxury they can't afford. The body is warm, there's no one else, the camera's rolling, so they say yes.

You hold yourself hostage when you give yourself the choice of only one person for the job. Not only because that person knows it and can misbehave accordingly. But also because they might literally be psychotic, incompetent, or both.

Don't make your choice between the lesser of two evils. Don't delude yourself into thinking that you can change them, or that everything will be different on your shoot. Give yourself time to find out the truth of people's work, satanic rituals, warrants out for their arrest, etc. Then give yourself enough time to keep looking.

If the potential crew member's references are over a year old, the reason may be burnout. Only time heals these wounds, and you want to make sure that the burn victim has had enough of it. If the latest car payment or mortgage payment is forcing them to work, they'll really be motivated for the first couple of weeks, but you can be sure that the burned out persona will resurface after that. There are a lot of damaged people in this business. It doesn't mean you have to work with them.

If a potential employee can't provide you with references from a project on their reel, chances are that this means:

- **It wasn't their work at all.** Anyone can say, "I am a xxx (fill in a crew position)." Anyone can read a book like this and pick up some catch phrases. Anyone can lie. If "anyone" includes you, remember that you'll be found out and your once and future reputation will burn. It is much better to get hired to assist the person whose job you aspire to and get on-the-job training. If that person drops out (which happens all the time), you get the job.

- **They didn't hold the position they claimed.** Title inflation makes a set dresser become an art director, while the assistant cameraman becomes cinematographer. The candidate's résumé should be logical given the fact that they're applying to work on a no-budget film. If their résumé says they've shot a $20 million feature, you should think they're either an idiot or a liar to want to work on your film. Look for people who are honest about their credits but are able to talk intelligently about what they did. Chances are, you can believe them if they explain how the scope of their input was broader than their modest title represents.

- **They had a bad relationship with the producer, director, or department head.** This is to be expected on occasional (i.e., one out of about ten) projects. But if someone doesn't want you to talk to people on a significant number of the films they have worked on, you have to ask yourself what they hope you won't find out.

When you're talking with someone the candidate has worked with, listen to what the reference person *isn't* saying, too. They may be protecting someone's reputation because it seems like a nice thing to do, because they feel sorry for them, or sorry—and maybe somewhat guilty—for the way things worked out.

If you feel there's something they're holding back, make it easier for them by providing the following yes or no questions about the candidate:

- What position did they actually hold? Make sure it's the one they said they held and that the responsibilities match.
- Was the person ever late? Always late?
- Did they stay for the whole shoot?

- Were they responsible for any money? Did you get all the receipts back? Were there any sudden budget surprises in their department or under their watch?
- When they had problems completing any part of the job, did they tell you right away? (Yes is the right answer.)
- When they had personal problems or anxieties about the job, did they tell you in time so you could work out a solution? (Yes is the right answer.)
- Did they ever lie to you? (There are very, very few exceptions that make this OK: namely, covering someone else's ass within reason, but not once it starts to seriously challenge the shoot.)
- Did they have problems with anyone on the crew? What kind?

And now for the essay question: What was your relationship with this person like at the beginning of the shoot, and what was it like at the end of your work together? What accounts for the change?

You can reduce this question to numerical format, too. Just ask them to assign, on a scale of one to ten, a number that rates the relationship at the start of their work together and a number that quantifies its state at the end.

Of course, you need to have good, reliable references on the person you're getting the references from. You'll want to cross-check what the potential hire says about their prior boss with what that person said. If there's a discrepancy, go back and ask the interviewee about them. Then it's up to you to decide who to trust—it could very well be the crew member.

▸▸94. GENIUS CAN BE MORE TROUBLE THAN IT'S WORTH.

We make a distinction between true and false genius.

The true geniuses we've worked with are also the most humble and generous and hardworking people we've ever met. They are so close to the power and beauty and mystery of the world that they live in a state of respectful awe. They know so much because they are always seeking to learn. They are interested in you, and what you know, because they have the sensitivity to recognize difference and appreciate it. They crave to know about the things you know, and the things you and only you can teach them.

It's the false geniuses you'll have problems with. In order to protect their (fragile) reputation as "genius," they will pretend to know things they don't know, will be afraid to ask questions, afraid to acknowledge your knowledge, and feel a total panic when things go out of their control.

These people are more invested in protecting their reputation than in doing the work. They'll need constant, exorbitant attention to and acknowledgment for their genius. They'll act like they're doing you a favor for showing up.

A false genius thinks it's his way or no way. He chooses to work on a film for the primary purpose of showcasing his own work. The true genius chooses your project to do work that can reflect both of you and, as such, be something totally new, which no one has ever dreamed or seen before. Some people have a genius for collaboration. They are infinitely more valuable to your film than someone who has a genius for doing only one thing, and is threatened or thrown off by the needs and contributions of other people, including you.

A true genius is interested and unafraid of new challenges because they pose a chance to find new solutions and to grow. The false genius has a hard time in learning environments because they point out what she doesn't know and make her feel vulnerable.

Emotional intelligence is the kind of genius you want. A genius of emotional intelligence who isn't especially trained in camera work would probably come up with better stuff than a genius of lighting who is challenged in the areas of empathy and human connection.

15

HIRE THE ACTORS WITH
THE SHINIEST SHOES

▶▶ 95. DON'T BELIEVE THE HEAD SHOTS.

Remember that your actors are there to convey the emotional dimension of your film. Otherwise you could just scroll your script's text up on the screen and be done with it. The actor is who we as an audience have to be willing to be for at least ninety minutes. We have to imagine that it would be appealing to bathe ourselves in his experience whether he's Hannibal Lecter or Harriet the Spy. The right actor makes your character so alive that he takes on a life beyond what you put on the page.

Head shots are, at best, just a source of contact information for actors in more or less the right age range. What makes an actor right is the proper match of their interior dimensions, not their exterior appearance. Wait for the alchemical reaction that happens when the right person reads for the role. You will feel the shift. The story will come alive.

▶▶ 96. HIRE THE WINNERS. THE LOSERS
WILL SEEK TO DESTROY YOU.

Actors don't just dramatize their lives through their roles but through their lives.

We all do. Find yourself in the same relationships over and over again, reliving the same version of pain? Coincidence? Probably not.

The familiar is comfortable. It's the logic and the lure behind habits. The person used to getting attention from negative feedback will seek out situations to get more. It can be more comfortable to re-create a condition you know well than cope with a new one, even if it's more promising. Winners, who are used to winning, tend to succeed regularly, as if by—indeed, by way of—habit. The same goes for losers.

In the relatively few hours you'll spend together, you just won't have time to heal their pain, make up for their childhood wounds, bolster their work ethic, and draw out their hidden talents. Film doesn't give you the same chance for on-the-job Gestalt therapy as theater might. Too many people are standing around being paid for that to be a financially responsible work style. The actors themselves may not be able to give you more time than what you get on the set. If you're working with SAG actors, on waiver from union pay scale to work on your film, you still need to work with SAG's other rules, which dictate, essentially, no free rehearsals. Even if the actor is willing to rehearse with you "under the table," you won't have enough time to fundamentally change them or their work. Just as change in people is incremental, change to the performance of the less gifted actor happens within a certain range only.

Anaïs Nin said that we don't see things as they are, but rather, we see things as we are. Choose people who see themselves, and the world, in the affirmative. Hire the winners—literally, the ones with the shiniest shoes. The ones who come on time, dress neatly, and have the solid positive attitude that affords them self-respect. Hire these actors and your work together will be shaped by a common determination to make something good.

Hire a loser, and you may find that the very promise of success causes him disarming stress. If you're leading a production of successful people toward an evident success, the self-identified, if closeted, loser may panic. Lost in this unfamiliar environment, and totally uncertain about what to do when faced with success, the loser will create a situation at which to fail.

More than likely, the drama(s) he creates will affect more than him. Misery loves company, and the loser's poor attitude will engage cast and crew, whose vulnerability to it will increase in times of stress.

While the rock-solid winners won't give in to the petty dramas, they will lose respect for you when *you* do. They'll think, "Why should we pay for Joe Loser's problems just because the director can't get him to behave?" And they'll be right.

▶▶ 97. YOUR FIRST LOOK'S YOUR BEST.

You gave everyone the same instructions about your audition and, without knowing it, set up a terrific context to compare work styles. Once you've given out the info regarding time, place, nature of the role, etc., the rest is up to them. If they blow the basics, it's because they don't believe they have control over their lives.

Here are a few audition firsts that will probably not be lasts:

- Late for the audition? She'll be late to the set.
- Getting that slightly lecherous, creepy vibe from him? It's probably not your imagination.
- Ego flaring up? She's starting a fight you'll continue later.
- Got lost and blamed you for bad directions? Everyone else got here.
- Irritated about having to wait? Do you think this will be the last time?
- Doesn't take your direction? Questions why you're giving an adjustment? Who's the director here?

We've found that all you have to do is turn the camera on and leave it on, and people will tell you everything you need to know about them. Same thing with an audition, only you are the camera. The actor walks in, having never met you before. But having imagined you. The fantasy they've created of you, without any real information, is by and large who you'll be to them. Sitting behind the closed door in an audition room, you are a blank slate representing authority.

An actor will walk in with his prior relationship to authority and paste it onto you. The family is the first experience most people have of collaboration and teamwork. A person's relationship to authority often comes out of the way power was wielded or shared in that context. Does she fear it or does she have a good relationship to it? During the audition, stay as neutral as possible, and try to determine who you represent to them in the familial power paradigm: mother, father, sister, brother, husband, wife, etc.

The actor-director relationship is like a temporary marriage. You two are going to be in a position to push and probe each other's emotional buttons. While your time together will be brief, the results will be recorded for eternity on film. Which is more than you can say for most marriages.

For the audition, use exercises that reflect your work style. If you like to talk about a part, do. If you want their ideas, try to get them. Try out what it's like to give them an adjustment, even if they got it exactly how you wanted it the first time. If you use analogies ("Do X as if Y") or "games" when directing actors in your work, try them now. These exercises will reflect the conditions under which you enjoy working, and reveal whether your collaborative styles match.

▸▸98. GAS STATION CASTING.

Gas station casting is noticing who you pay attention to in your everyday life; it's noticing who the people are you'd go out of your way to watch. If you choose to go to a particular gas station or restaurant because of an individual who works there, then these quiet stars actually determine where you spend your money. Which is the elusive but real economic value of a movie star. Someone you'd pay to watch. Over someone else.

It's not a question of beauty.

It's more appropriate to speak in terms of sexy, and yet we don't quite mean that, either. Not literally. The talent agent Camille worked for in New York had only one question for Camille the mornings after he sent her to scout a showcase. "Anyone sexy?" he would ask matter-of-factly, when Camille thought she was supposed to be looking for acting talent.

When unknowns came into the office, the talent agent persisted: "Would you sleep with them?" he asked. Again, just as matter-of-factly. Gender, age, sexuality, etc., didn't matter. He didn't mean the question literally. But with it he was teaching her to look for star quality, by zeroing in on what a star has in addition to and quite apart from ability. That quality may be their capacity to fascinate, to make you look, to make you keep looking, even as you don't know why. Charisma, which has to do with a fundamental, and often unconscious, confidence—has something to do with it. Integrity—a sense that they don't need to change for anything or anyone—may have everything to do with it.

Keep tabs on people like this when you find them. Take down their contact information. You may feel a bit "Hollywood" doing this, but goddammit, man, you're an independent filmmaker and you've got to be creative.

You don't know what a camera is going to do to someone. Some people look better and more interesting, some people less so, some people about the same. But you have to have someplace to start. You're halfway there when you've noticed someone's special quality. The something that makes them people you could watch for no good reason. Next, see if it remains intact on camera. Essentially, whether it's so inborn that even inevitable awkwardness can't interrupt it.

▶▶ 99. WHY MODELING TALENT DOESN'T NECESSARILY TRANSLATE TO THE MOVIE CAMERA.

Professional photographer Bob Ware has a great explanation. A model's talent involves being able to sum up an entire state of being in 1/250 of a second. Once she does, she is ready for the next frame. Problem is, for film there aren't just 36 frames per roll. Rather, there are 24 frames a second. A film performance needs to be continuous, at least the length of a take. It should be as monumentally (and deceptively) uneventful as breathing. It isn't a series of fireworks. It's the capacity to sit still and let things happen to you.

▶▶ 100. SILENT STAR REVISITED

Casting for nonspeaking roles, which is something you do a lot of when you can't afford a sync-sound camera, is a talent in and of itself.

If the whole film is nonsync, then you are going for the silent film standard of acting. Cast for the ability to play emotion through facial expression and motion—not voice. Some actors use their voice as their primary instrument of emotional expression, such that when they perform a nonspeaking role, they come off as thoroughly uninteresting and flat, while they seemed scintillating during their audition monologue. Do not allow yourself to get seduced by an actor's great verbal skill if this is not what you need for your film. If you need voice-over for your character, the actor does not need to be the one who actually does it. Since you will record the voice separately and at a later time, you can cast separately for it.

One audition strategy for the actor with no lines is to give them a direction that must be expressed subtextually through a given action. Thinking about a war memory while cooking eggs, for example.

Actors with small nonspeaking parts are technically extras, but this moniker is deceiving. It implies optional. Usually they are not. Often they are key. They can make or break a film or a scene. They require careful casting and directing. Unfortunately, directors and producers don't realize this soon enough and leave casting extras to a production assistant to manage or even just do cattle calls from extra agencies. Bad idea unless we are talking about a huge crowd scene.

Ever see someone who is an extra just destroy all sense of credibility to the scene or project? No matter how wonderful the rest of the scene might have been, that person was either too interesting or too interested. It takes some skill to be just interesting and interested enough.

▶▶101. CAN THEY SAY "NO-BUDGET FILM"?

There's no career to be made as a student film star. For actors, student films are a means to an end. But they need to treat the job as a reasonable end in itself if you're going to have a good working relationship and get good work from them.

As with crew, you want to make sure you're choosing actors who have something tangible and realistic to gain:

- A young actor (child or young adult) who doesn't have experience (or tape), but truly has potential
- A promising actor whose agent wants to give them experience in anticipation of paying work
- A theater actor or a stand-up comedian who wants to move into film
- A TV actor who wants to try a role that goes against his or her type
- A trained actor getting back into acting after, perhaps, a stint as a paid member of society. They may have enough money and real-world validation to hold them for a while, but also have a real desire to try acting again. For which they need new tape of themselves. Enter your film.
- An actor who shares special concern for the theme or cause that your film expresses. In other words, who truly wishes to work for the cause.
- Actors who truly crave the same thing you do—a sense of community. The chance to join a friendship circle of other filmmakers who are doing interesting films and may cast them as a result of working on your project.

On the other hand, genres of actors less likely to work out include:

- Actors bitter that their agent sent them on this and not on paying jobs. Convinced that their agent is doing jack for them and furious that they don't have the cachet or credits to get a better one.
- Actors afraid to work without pay because they think it means they're losers
- Older actors who have been trying this for most of their life but, it eventually becomes apparent, never succeeded for reasons of lack of talent, lack of concentration, or lack of professionalism
- Male actors who are just barely starting to become aware that they missed their chance to play a leading man, and resent you for casting them as an older guy, or in a character role
- Ditto for women
- Actors with bad habits with no interest in changing them. If you're set on curing someone of bad habits, young people offer your best chances. The habits have had less time to sink into the fabric of who they are. Funny, if it wasn't terribly sad, are the stories of actors refusing to cooperate because "Johnny Cassavetes" didn't do it this way. How many actors did he work with, for God's sake?

▶▶102. CHOOSE A CHILD ACTOR WHOSE PARENTS LOVE TO DRIVE.

Remember that children:

- Don't drive
- Need constant on-set supervision (indeed, by law)
- Can get exhausted easily and unpredictably
- Can get weirded out or upset by things you couldn't have anticipated

The only person who can deal with these issues are the parents, so choose some that seem grown-up enough to do so. Not all are. Sometimes what makes the successful child actor so good is their talent to *act* like a kid. Playing out roles they don't get a chance to play at home. They can cry like a little boy or laugh like a little girl because they've seen other kids do it and wanted to try it themselves.

Melissa (not her real name), age eight, would call us from the freeway to get directions when her mother and car had breakdowns. During breaks she helped with her mother's community college math homework, and asked us for extra help when she didn't know the answer.

Hire a child actor and you're literally hiring their parents. The parent(s) join your set and wield (or inflict, as the case might be) as much influence as any actor or crew person. As much as they may act out, parents answer to no one. Not to you, not to producers. They're parents.

▶▶103. A *LITTLE* BIT OF STAGE PARENT IS A GOOD THING.

With every generation is born a new era of stage parent. The charming thing is how they will all tell you, both early and often, that they're "not like those other stage parents."

In many ways, you should be happy if they are. Kids need someone to look out for them. If they're lucky enough to have someone who's actively responsible on their behalf, consider the alternative, and have respect for the parent's efforts.

A film set is a dangerous place, especially for kids. Lights could fall on them or they could get electrocuted—for starters. Then there's also poisoning, tripping on cables, getting run over by a truck, or slammed on the head by a lift gate—take your pick of industrial accidents, the possibilities are endless. Your crew should work to child-proof the set, but there's only so much they can do to keep a kid from picking up a hot barn door off a light and searing the fingerprints off his little six-year-old hand.

The thing you can and absolutely must control is the behavior of cast and crew. This starts, of course, with no swearing. Try the "put a quarter in a hat for every bad word" game and you'll end up with extra pizza at the wrap party. It makes us cringe just to have to mention it, but you need to be on the lookout for any hint of sexual innuendo, harassment, or abuse to these kids. Be paranoid. The best thing that can happen is that you're wrong.

If the child has scenes with grown-up actors, audition the adults in scenes with children and cast the ones who know how to behave around kids. They should intuitively know to break out of character between scenes and act with respect, interest, and protective warmth with the kids in the cast. On the other extreme, we remember a terrible audition improvisation gone wrong. The so-called grown-up was so chillingly verbally abusive with the child that we had to stop the audition, escort the woman out, and spend the rest of the afternoon assuring the child that the woman was only acting.

Parents have a big job. Be glad when they take it seriously. One director friend lost an argument to a young actress's mother and still thanks her for it. For the sake of the scene, he was trying to make the girl cry. For the sake of "reality" he was bullying her, and it was working. The girl's mother, standing by on the set, stopped him. As a mother, she said, she couldn't see him doing that to her daughter. A child. Her child.

No film is worth a child, or anyone, having emotional scars. You know it's true, even if in the midst of directorial glee you have to be reminded sometimes. Our friend was glad the child actor's mother put her foot down. The scene was just as good without tears. Good enough to get the girl work in television. Which, with the benefits of her mother's protection, she had no reason to fear.

▶▶104. THE JUNIOR CASTING DIRECTOR IS YOUR NEW BEST FRIEND.

If casting is ninety percent of directing, as is commonly said, then it pays to have a casting director, since they improve your chance of hiring a great cast by a hundred percent or more.

They know who the up-and-coming actors are because they've helped to create them by passing on the names of actors they believe in to agents they believe can best help them. If luck works in your favor, these actors may break by the time your film comes out, giving it that much more visibility and cachet. Or your casting director can use your film as a chance to get a new discovery seen by agents. This happened with Karen Church's discovery of Jena Malone, who Camille cast in her student project. Jena has gone on to work with Susan Sarandon, Glenn Close, Julia Roberts, Anjelica Houston, Goldie Hawn, Kevin Costner . . . the list goes on.

Casting directors serve as friendly go-betweens to actors' agents, promoting you and lending credibility to your project. Agents take their calls even when the work doesn't pay because they need the casting directors to be responsive to them and their clients when the job does pay.

Casting directors can prescreen dozens of actors and show you only the most promising. They know talent when they see it. They've seen a lot of what it isn't. They have convenient offices for your auditions, to which actors tend to show up on time. They'll help you get back-up choices if actors fall through, even at a moment's notice.

Casting directors know who is working and who isn't. They know how much people are making and who is really and truly desperate or available. They bring the six degrees of separation we all have to anyone famous down to two.

Before you worry that there is no way you could afford to hire a casting director, rest assured that with the right approach, you can work with a casting director for free.

Casting is one of the few professions in Hollywood that still works with an apprentice system. Assistants are selected carefully and work under the wing of the lead casting director, gradually taking over more direct responsibility for casting a film on their own. Today's casting assistants are truly tomorrow's casting directors. While they may do a great deal of administrative work, they are never just secretaries. Even in their training-wheel days, they have access to the same agents, phone numbers, and lists of talent as do their bosses and mentors.

Casting assistants often work for the sake of experience (this means for free, plus office expenses) on student films. All with the full authority and support of their bosses, who see the projects as an under-the-radar way for the assistant to practice their fledgling casting skills and instincts. Then there's also the possibility that if the relationship works out with you, it can continue through increasingly ambitious and (eventually) paying films you may produce or direct.

But what truly compels many a casting assistant to work on nonpaying projects is (as bizarre as it sounds): they're nice. The profession succeeds in attracting people who have a genuine love for what they do, and are in the job for the right reason: they like actors. Casting directors are among the few in the business who really and truly do.

Although actors who haven't had the pleasure of knowing a casting director may find this hard to believe, casting directors are truly actors' advocates. They enjoy meeting them and enjoy the chance to cast them in their first films. Casting directors serve as meta-agents, looking out for a broad group of favorite actors, without the pressure or distortion of commission. Your film gives them a chance to cast actors they appreciate, regardless of their name value or experience.

How can you find one of these benevolent individuals of the junior variety? First, look for the names of casting directors they would be working for. That is, identify casting directors whose work you admire.

Pay attention to the casting director's name in the credits of films whose casts you like, especially those with a population, or quality, in common with the film you're planning, or with a charismatic collection of fantastic unknowns. If the film is out of theaters, pick up the video cassette box and find their name in the credits.

Finding the assistant is essentially as simple as calling the casting director's office and speaking to the person who answers the phone. Finding a current office phone number can be the tricky part. Casting directors often move their office to their current project's production suites; therefore their phone numbers are constantly changing. The Casting Society of America can help you find their current number. If the casting director has moved on from the last listing, you can ask whoever picks up the phone at the old number what film the casting director left to work on next. Then track down a contact number through the studio or production company producing the film.

The next part is up to you, and attention to etiquette goes without saying. Do your research about the casting director's company's work, and be clear about why you're calling. You're making a film with important roles for older Asian actors, for example, and you were very impressed with the sensitivity of their office's casting on "x" film. You're a student, making a twenty-minute film that starts shooting in three months. You're wondering if any of the assistants in their office ever work for free on student projects. You are, of course, happy to pay for all office expenses incurred. You'd love to drop off a script and a tape of your previous work.

Then you're off to a good start.

This part is obvious, too, but just in case: treat the person with the utmost respect. Their opinions are informed and their work professional. It's OK to disagree with their suggestions, but share why. Remain open to their ideas, especially the unusual ones. Michael Katcher, a prominent television casting director, agreed to cast Camille's first USC film, a story based on her family. His choice for Camille's mother, Caitlin O'Heaney, a freckled Irish redhead and avid horsewoman, didn't have the slightest resemblance to Camille's blond, not-so-athletic French mother. Until she acted. Then Caitlin became Babette, a woman that neither she nor Michael had ever met. At the screening, even Babette, who's not one to hold back the truth, thought so, too. Enough to cry with a feeling of recognition.

We wish you the same unique pleasure of sharing your most elusive casting dreams with someone who might understand them even better than you do.

▶▶105. QUICK REJECTION IS THE KOSHER WAY.

You think you're doing actors a favor by stringing them along. Drawing out the inevitable moment when you tell them you've selected someone else. To let them feel *almost* wanted until you tell them that they're not. It's patronizing and cruel. By protecting them in this bogus way, you're suggesting that they need to be protected in this bogus way. Treating actors professionally means giving them an answer as soon as you know it yourself.

We're not saying tell them while they're in the room. Call the next day. But don't wait any longer. If you're truly horrified, ask a fellow filmmaker to make the calls, and return the favor on their next film. If you're working with a casting director, she will make the calls, which is another reason why she should be your next best friend. Camille once found the only way to do it herself was to invest in a roll of quarters and make all the calls systematically from a pay phone. She wouldn't allow herself to leave until all the calls were made. She got through all of them in one session, with the de facto urgency you get when you're standing in the cold on a night street.

Still can't bring yourself to make the call(s)? Remember that while telling them they didn't get the part will be hard, think how much harder it would be to tell them every day that you don't like their performance.

It's OK to leave a message on their machine. Rejection can be easier to take through the mediation of a dumb machine. For this reason you may want to plan the run of phone calls in the middle of the day when people are out.

Write out your message and practice it until you can come off as calm and positive. You don't want to pass along any stress or drama, particularly since they're the ones with the right to these emotions, not you. In a warm tone, start by thanking them for the time, attention, and interest they gave you and your project. Next, share that you're glad to have met them. Finally, say something like "unfortunately, it's just not the right match for this project." Conclude with another note of thanks for giving you the chance to meet them. Feel free to leave your number in the message if you feel compelled to. We've never been called back for further details.

If the actor answers the phone, however, proceed as above. Don't worry that you'll spend a long and painful time talking. No one wants to draw out their own rejection, and they'll find a way to close the conversation quickly. You'll actually be surprised at how gracious and strong people will be. Often they'll even thank you for calling, adding that so many people don't.

If a roommate picks up, don't leave a message or your name. It's not polite to leave bad news through someone else, who might deliver it without the slightest note of gentleness. On the other hand, it's rude and cruel to leave your name and number and ask to be called back just so you can deliver bad news. Instead, make a point of calling again and either catching them or falling on the mercifully impersonal machine.

Do the job quickly and let go of the anxiety. The notion that you are feeling their pain is presumptuous and flatters you into believing that you have more power than you do. Remember that there are other, and hopefully bigger, fish for them to fry. Let them go fishing.

16

THE EMPEROR'S PARADE

▶▶106. PRETEND THE PRODUCTION IS MOVING EVEN WHEN IT ISN'T.

Newton's first law of motion: objects at rest remain at rest, while objects in motion remain in motion. Inertia is an object's resistance to change.

From Newton's first law you could wonder how objects at rest ever get moving. You may wonder the same about your film. Newton's second law of motion defines force as a push that when applied to a mass causes the object to accelerate.

It's harder to move people than objects, particularly without the magic force of money. In your case, the push may be a white lie, designed to lure people into believing that your film is already moving, so they will get up and move with it.

No one wants to be the first one to jump on the bandwagon— riding around town like an idiot, singing to himself, and banging on a coffee can. That first person on your film's bandwagon has got to be you. Indeed, no one wants to be the second person to jump on the bandwagon, either. This would put them in the position of having to share your embarrassment as you ride around town singing to yourself and banging on a coffee can.

You'll have to convince investors, actors, crew, and everyone else that they're not the first and not the only ones to think that what you are doing is destined for greatness. You have to persuade them to believe that they are merely joining in on a foregone conclusion. This minimizes their risk of exposure.

Maintaining the appearance of constant forward motion on your project gives it a chance at becoming a reality. The stone soup parable works here:

A poor man came to town with nothing to eat. Instead of begging for food, he promised he had something to give. He claimed he would make soup with a stone. People brought him a pot, kindling, and water. He provided the rock. As the villagers watched the water boil, the man remarked that the soup would be even better with carrots. Carrots were brought. Indeed, the soup smelled better. He added that it would be even more delicious with onions. Gladly, onions were brought. A chicken, he said, would really make a difference. Enter the chicken. By the time the water had simmered for a few hours of this routine, it was thick with flavorful offerings. Indeed, all who tasted it found it delicious. All were amazed that you could make soup this good with nothing but a stone.

Baby, you've got the stone: it's the time and place your film is happening. And, of course, the script. Set those in stone, and you'll have a pot in which to put the contributions people bring.

▶▶ 107. PUTTING NEWTON'S SECOND LAW INTO PRACTICE.

Without the push of deadlines, objects at rest—students or office workers—wouldn't get into motion. With a deadline you assert what the future will look like. And since nobody knows the future, who's going to argue with you when you say that the production's starting June 1?

If *you're* in any doubt that your production will start on this date, spend some money. This is equivalent to having a non-refundable plane ticket for going home at Christmas, even when you're still in the midst of three term papers and you have writer's block. You can stare at the ticket and know that somehow, no matter what, you're going to be on that plane in just seven hours. Meaning that the papers will be done by then, too. Similarly, one

ake the prophecy of your film's start date self-fulfilling is
ocation or a camera package for that date. Or buy a plane
ck home, if that's where you're going to shoot the film.

Now your production is an object in motion. To keep up with
it, you and others need to get moving, too. Once the perception
ignites that your production's "train" is moving, it can be (wonder-
fully) hard to stop it.

▸▸108. IF YOU'RE NOT GOOD AT PRETENDING, GET A PRODUCER WHO IS.

Linguists argue that the idea of a thing, embodied by a name, gives
birth to it. As in Genesis 1:3: "Let there be light. And there was
light." Regardless of the physical existence of light or of God, the
idea, and naming of light gives it form—if only in the mind.

On a much more modest scale than the power society assigns
to God, we invest certain mere mortals with the power to perform
what linguists call "speech acts"—creating events, objects, and legal
entities through speech. An umpire only has to say, "Play ball," and
players do. A minister says, "With the power vested in me, I now
pronounce you husband and wife," and they are. "We declare these
to be United States," wrote a bunch of guys on July 4, 1776, and
we were. Magic words. With an effect not unlike like abracadabra.

You should choose a producer that naturally has this kind of
power. The kind who says, "We are making this film. Production
starts next week," and is believed. Someone with the power for self-
fulfilling prophecy.

All films, even those with much more money at hand than
yours, are really just conceptual art until they're shot, edited, and
screened for an audience. In the days and weeks of preproduction
and shooting, they exist as nothing more than a bundle of plans
and desires. Someone—starting with you but preferably backed up
with someone else—has to believe that all these things will end up
as a film. That's part of what people mean by "having the vision."
Completing a film requires skills much more basic than artistic

choice. It requires the faith to see the light at the end of the tunnel. Actually, the will to see the light before you even create the tunnel.

A producer is, among other things, a salesperson who transfers the belief that the film will happen. No one wants to invest money, time, and interest in something that won't ever materialize. They want to see what they gave put to tangible use, and maybe even get it back at the end.

▶▶109. KEEPING ALL YOUR FISH ON THE HOOK.

You must learn to be skilled at sustaining interest and involvement without being untruthful. This gets difficult when things really aren't going so well, or really aren't going anywhere at all.

Try this: it's not a lie if you believe.

OK, we know. Some will say this is the most stupid definition of a lie ever. Talk about convenient. But think about it. When you walk into someone's office and say, "This story will be a huge hit," are you telling the truth? You have no idea. It might be true. Or history might prove you wrong (and, OK, if you want to be harsh about it, a liar).

But the moment you stop believing, they'll stop believing in you. At any point in the creative and business timeline people can get cold feet and jump ship. It's your job to keep them on board and to plow ahead past your own self-doubt to victory.

▶▶110. THE ETIQUETTE OF POSTPONING.

There is an etiquette to keeping the fish on your hook happy.

Don't make them share your embarrassment about the fact that your plans are delayed. People really don't want to know about the depressing details of why things are not happening. Tell them what they need to know and move on.

If the financial model of the film changes, let the "fish" you're holding know, and let them make their own decision. They may or may not fit anymore, but if they stay, you've just given yourself a fresh start. Reevaluate who can still benefit in the new configuration. Let them off the hook if they don't have anything to gain.

Keep the ones you can confide in. These are the people whom you can share everything with, including your doubt. These are called: your friends.

Don't keep fish on the hook that you'd just as soon toss back. Don't lead people on in association with a project only to tell them down the line, when things begin to work out for the production, that they're no longer needed. If you feel like you're leading someone on and keeping them around as a placeholder until you can find or afford someone else you'd really rather work with, don't. You're only planting the seeds of enmity.

Postponing can bring its own surprises and rewards. People's involvement and influence on the project can grow over time and assume an importance that is increasingly prized. That storyboard artist that you brought on last year from the community college drawing class to help you get investors may now be a digital designer at Industrial Light & Magic who wants to help the project by getting Lucasfilm to donate services. Tadpoles can turn into frogs and sometimes princes.

17

DONUTS, RED VINES, AND KEEPING THE CREW TOGETHER: THE CARE AND FEEDING OF THE SET

▶▶111. ACCEPT CONFLICT. IT MEANS PEOPLE CARE.

Clear and open conflict is the sign of a healthy set. Silence, interrupted by the occasional slammed door, is the sign that the creative process is stuck in the loathsome black hole of personality conflict.

There's an important difference between intellectual disagreement and personality conflict. When you and your friend argue over a movie, it's based on your respect for each other and each other's ideas. No one's trying to win the argument, really. You'd be happy to keep it going in order to get at what each of you truly believes.

Passionate arguments take energy. They're worth having only when you feel you have something at stake, something you don't want to lose. Including each other's respect. The reason breaking up is so hard to do is that you both still care. If you didn't, you'd just shake hands and walk away.

Arguments with people you don't respect don't last long. You end up just *telling* them what to do. Or, if they've got the power, you'll probably icily accept their directions, then quietly find a way to sabotage them in return.

In scripts, the best way to get your characters to express their beliefs is to engage them in an argument. On the set, constructive conflict lets people come clean about ideas they may not have really understood until they expressed them.

Try to get yourself and your crew to understand the chapter

from high school physics that explains: there are good and bad types of friction, it just depends on what you need to get done. Bad friction includes the kind that happens between your car's engine parts. Changing kinetic energy to useless heat, this friction causes your car to lose efficiency. On the other hand, if it wasn't for friction, it would be impossible for your car's tires to push against the pavement, and your car would go nowhere. Race car tires have no treads—in order to have *more* friction and more speed. You should strive to get your crew to move each other toward more creative solutions through the friction of their ideas, while avoiding the energy loss caused by the friction of personalities.

How? Here's another analogy from physics. Concentrated stress, such as the weight of a 140-pound woman channeled through a single spike heel on your face, causes damage and pain. More so than that same weight distributed on two flat heels. Likewise, while lying on a single nail is torture of biblical proportions, lying on a bed of nails (where stress is distributed) is perfectly possible. False prophets do it all the time.

Diffuse the power of any single person's argument (read: spike heel, single nail) by taking it out of the realm of one-on-one conflict. Encourage group discussions. Make everyone responsible for ideas and opinions. Turn arguments into debates in which several crew members participate, and you dilute the personal sting of an argument aimed like an arrow.

▶▶112. YOUR FRIENDS WILL ENJOY PRODUCTION ABOUT AS MUCH AS THEY LOVE HELPING YOU MOVE. LET THEM OFF THE HOOK.

Since working on a set isn't any more fun or rewarding than schlepping mattresses to a truck, your friends have to have love for you that's as warm as your grandparents' or as hot as a lover's.

In addition to the hard work production demands, the underlying problem of getting friends and lovers to truly help is that they can't see the point of it all. When you're in the midst of the storm that is your set, you can see nothing but things you need to do. To someone who's not familiar with the work, and the linear sequences it needs to go through in order to get accomplished, the whole thing seems like the eye of the storm. Like nothing's really happening. Or whatever's happening is happening ridiculously slowly.

Most didn't come to give so much as they came to get. Validation and appreciation from you, and some kind of backstage-at-the-rock-concert glamour. Instead, all they find are a crumpled crew and a messy craft service table with a vague moldy smell. They hang on, expecting the glamour to show up. They stand around with a small expectant smile, as if waiting for someone to pour them a martini.

You act delighted that they're there, you thank them more than once. They ask, of course, if there's something they can do. You have other things to worry about than what they can do without any training or fundamental commitment to getting their hands dirty. Finally you come up with something: make some more coffee. They do this very seriously, as if Patton's army depended on them. Three minutes later, they're done.

Is there anything else they can do? You make the mistake of handing them off to the A.D. to find something. This won't do. It's the equivalent of assigning them to the junior secretary pool when they've come to lounge in the executive suite. Being your friend, they naturally assume, gives them the privilege to jump through the corporate ranks. To go straight for the glamour and the glamorous work.

If only there was any of that to give them. Better you thank them, say how nice it was of them to drop by, and let them be on their way to a nice brunch and the Sunday paper.

▶▶113. NEVER, EVER UNDERESTIMATE THE IMPORTANCE OF COFFEE.

Your production is no time to cut people off from their not-so-good habits. They need cigarettes, they need coffee, don't argue with them.

The only two sure-thing pleasures of the day for your crew are the smell of good coffee when they get to the set, and the comfort of their car radio and a smoke on their way back home.

Start the day out the only right way. Make the coffee yourself, and make it good. Get there early enough to make a pot for the thermos and another pot for the machine. Don't be caught short. Once those two pots are done, start the decaf. If you don't have this down before the first person shows up, you'll both just spend the first few minutes staring at the pot as it slowly drips to its conclusion.

Buy the most expensive kind and let people see the packages. If someone wants some other expensive brand, get that. Don't forget the real cream, sugar, Sweet'n Low, and the stuff that comes in the blue packages. These are the cheapest drug you can buy your crew, so go all out. Just about the only compliment you might get to hear about your set is "good coffee." You'll also never hear the end of it if it isn't.

▶▶114. DON'T BELIEVE ANYONE WHEN THEY ASK FOR HEALTH FOOD. BUT BUY IT ANYWAY.

Film = stress. Stress = cravings for comfort. In America, comfort = food.

Comfort food is a matter of individual neurosis, but it really rarely means carrots and sprouts. Think of the food groups you curl up with in bed with after a breakup: ice cream, chocolate chip cookies, fried things, doughy textures.

People may want to be healthy, but in times of stress, they need something else. When it's between want and need, need wins. So, when you're shopping for the carrots they insisted on having, don't forget to stop at the Hostess display.

▶▶115. HAVE THE FOOD THE ACTORS REQUEST.

Actors can create meaning out of the words you wrote, and on bad days they can find meaning in anything. A wounded actor can find disagreeable subtext in the brand of cream cheese you bought.

Not to mention the following faux pas you didn't know you made:

- Since there's no special place for them to change, you must not respect their dignity.
- Since there's no special place for them to wait between takes, you must not respect their process.
- Since there's no one assigned to take care of their wardrobe, you must not respect their instrument.
- Since you didn't buy herbal tea for the set, you must not care about their health.
- Since you didn't plan macrobiotic meals like they asked you to, you must not care about their health, and you must not be listening to them.

If an actor goes to the trouble of expressing a concern, either directly or subtly, as a subtle actor can, it means they have one. They expect a solution, or at least a sincere reaction from you. Remember that theirs is a fragile, difficult, and sometimes frightening job. Regardless of the role, they have to show their insides to a camera and, by extension, to possibly millions of people. Since addressing many of their complaints and perceived slights may be beyond your budget and control, having the food an actor requests is an easy way to show you care.

▶▶116. KEEP THE CANDY AWAY FROM THE KIDS. THE OVER-TWELVE KIND, TOO.

John Waters' film *Pecker* features a hysterical and truthful portrayal of a girl hooked on sugar with the conviction of heroin. Drugs determine desires and leave little room for autonomy. Sugar is an over-the-counter drug that you really want to moderate, or suffer the side effects.

A shooting day can easily take on the temporal dimensions of a waking slumber party. While it may seem fun to score more candy than you've had since the Halloween of '83, you'll all pay the price.

O.D., and you'll get manic, maybe even start throwing things. Just as suddenly you'll hit the wall and feel, all at once, exhausted, nauseous, gross, cranky, and ready to go home. Instead of being able to call your parents to pick you up the morning after the sleepover, you'll have to keep working. Together.

Film production work days start at twelve hours. Concentration becomes a game of diminishing returns, but especially if the food's working against you and your crew. Candy and soda highs are sweet, sharp, and short. Their hangovers and side effects' half-lives are long. Keep an eye on the kids and provide a kind of warning-label approach to the grown-ups, including yourself.

▶▶ 117. BRING THE DONUTS TO THE SET YOURSELF.

You're sleep-deprived and you're working harder than anyone else. Try as you might, you'll never get the crew to feel sorry for you. They're too busy feeling sorry for themselves.

This is no time to rehearse the role of prima donna director. Overworked crew, sweating without glory and without pay, have no tolerance for bullshit. Even if your job is harder, you're also the only one who stands to get any public reward.

Everyone is working for free, and you can't underestimate how fragile that makes them, and how worthy of your gratitude. Even if you've knocked yourself out by doing the big things—finding the location, juggling the schedule, rewriting scenes—it's on the not-so-little things that you'll be judged. So, say good morning every day and thank you every evening. Lloyd Kaufman, the president of Troma Films, is known and appreciated by the overworked, underpaid citizens (i.e., staff) of Tromaville (i.e., the company's Hell's Kitchen walk-up) for his irrepressible urge to end every request with "Thank you very much." We visited Tromaville in the heart of a New York heat wave, when the building's air conditioning had broken down. The office staff labored under a blanket of sweat, making any request for work seem unreasonable. Lloyd made them anyway, with his anachronistic politesse accompanying every request. Instead of screaming, the staff chuckled at the persistence of his courtly behavior even under such conditions.

Learn from Lloyd and show your appreciation for each and every person, individually and sincerely, early and often. Be the first one on the set and the last one to leave. Bring the donuts. It's literally the least you can do.

▶▶118. DON'T LEAVE A MESS FOR ANYONE ELSE TO CLEAN UP.

The best way to get people to work harder is to jump into the ditch with them and grab a shovel. On a no-budget film, where no one is getting paid, if you don't lead by example, you'll have no one left to lead.

18

GRACE UNDER PRESSURE: DIRECTING UNDER FIRE

▶▶119. GOOD REASONS TO CALL "CUT" . . .

1. The boom is making a guest star appearance.

2. A bystander is making a guest star appearance, and is more interesting than anything else in the frame.

3. The sound tape ran out.

4. The actor isn't faking that scream.

. . . and good reasons not to.

1. The sound people already ran out of tape before, and you don't want to be further embarrassed in front of your actor because you still want her/his willingness to do another take.

2. The kid is crying. Zoom in for a close-up. You can use these authentic tears in a scene where the kid's supposed to cry.

3. You've actually got the camera turned on someone who doesn't know they're in the scene and is doing a great job—naturally.

4. The camera never went on. Don't tell the actors. You didn't waste any film, so just do "another" take. Just make sure you turn on the camera this time.

5. The actor in your horror film is doing a better job of look-ing expectant, confused, or anxious about when you're going to call cut than he did about the monster. Keep rolling.

6. The second after everyone's finished talking is the all-impor-tant reaction shot you'll need to edit the scene. It provides the essential reaction shot and resting space necessary for closure, like a period at the end of a sentence.

7. Positive rather than negative reinforcement works best with some actors. If this is the case for yours, don't ever cut because a performance is bad, because it will only get worse on the next take.

▸▸ 120. DON'T GOSSIP, ON PAIN OF EVERYONE ELSE DOING IT ABOUT YOU.

People who feel cheated, who feel they haven't gotten all the atten-tion or benefits they expected, gossip. Gossip, like stealing, is a reac-tion to loss. It's a chance to recover something promised and therefore to collect on the faith given to the promise.

If you gossip about cast or crew, you do indeed default on the only promise you made: to value their work, their effort, and them. Cast and crew's dignity and confidence are already on trial because they're working for free. Now that you've broken the promise, they're owed something: their own, if not your, respect. The up-shot: they'll gossip, or steal, or both, until they get enough back.

If you're being gossiped about for no reason, don't give into this revenge response, however. It's a vicious cycle, to nowhere. The only protection you have is taking the high road. Moral authority and dig-nity are the only bridges you have out of this self-feeding vipers' den.

▸▸ 121. EMBARRASS THE ACTORS AND LOSE THE FILM.

A camera is like a truth serum. It strips all ordinariness, and all pro-tection, from whoever's in front of it. It also removes the clues and cues we get from other people that allow us all to behave, more or less, on autopilot. It finds out who we are.

Actors aren't acting, they're being themselves. Some part of their personality more than another part perhaps, but nevertheless fundamentally themselves.

They're naked, and they know it. Don't clap your hands.

Even if it's clear that the actor's emotionally naked, you both must pretend, together, that no one else can see it. Your job is to let them know that you know, and that you'll protect them from everyone else. You are the link between their world and the world of the crew, and you must perform this role without ever betraying them or their secrets. Do so and you break the bubble they need to do their work in. Where there's no trust, there's no performance.

If someone in the crew insults your actors in any way, you have to make a big show of responding and reprimanding. If you think there's a chance the crew member will do it again, you should fire them. Another insult or raised eyebrow and the actor, if he hasn't shut down already, will give you nothing more.

The cinematographer on one of our films brutally insulted the talented lead actress with a comment along the lines of: "If she could act, we would be done by now." The comment was totally unjustified, juvenile, and would have been bad enough on its own. But the truly disastrous thing was that it was broadcast loudly through the headphones we were all wearing. She heard. We lost the rest of that scene and would have lost much more if she hadn't been willing and able to push her terrible hurt and justified anger through her remaining scenes that day.

There are ironclad rules regarding the handling of actors that should never be breached:

- No criticizing performance
- No criticizing the actor's personality, talent, look, hair, body, eye shadow—anything about the actor at all
- No complaints about anything any of the actors ask for

- No dirty jokes, either. They're not nearly as funny when you're "naked."

▸▸122. PLANT THE CAMERA, CHANGE YOUR MIND LATER.

They're standing around, the entire crew. On pause, waiting for the answer to the only question that matters: where's the next shot?

Even if your shot list has been blown to hell, make a decision. Tell them anything, and they can get to work, concentrating on something more constructive than when you're going to get your head together. Meanwhile, you've bought yourself some time to figure out what your next shot really is.

They have no idea how you're going to use the placebo shot, so there's no reason they should criticize you. Of course, you have no idea how, or if, you'll use it, either. Which isn't to say that you won't. A film is ultimately made in the editing room.

With exceptions made for Hitchcock, Kubrick, and very few others, it's hubris to believe that you know the one and only place the camera needs to be at all times. It's standard Hollywood practice to shoot coverage, for God's sake. Meaning that even experienced directors know kind of where the camera should be, but not well enough to know where they should place all their bets.

▸▸123. THE CAST AND CREW NEED YOU TO SEEM STRONG EVEN MORE THAN YOU NEED TO BREAK DOWN.

Because filmmaking is stressful, it brings out people's basic (a.k.a. base) personalities. Most turn into children. They want to cry, they want to ask, "Are we there yet?," and they want to be taken care of. You will, too, since you'll have more stress on you than anyone else. But here's the unfair thing: as the director, you can't show it.

Your job is to be the parent. Mother, father, or both at once, depending on the situation. This isn't something that anyone is going to be aware of, and it's certainly not something you should talk about, but it's true.

Acting is such a difficult job, and a trying career, that we've concluded that a psychological dynamic must be at work. It's been said that many people become actors because they feel that one or both of their parents didn't love them enough. The mass love that big-screen success promises might be the antidote they're after à la Sally Field's plaintive cry, "You like me, you really like me!" on accepting her Academy Award. In the meantime, the rejection that's built into the job is oddly comfortable because it re-creates a familiar experience.

As the director, and the cast and crew's prime giver of validation or criticism, you're being set up. You're going to be treated as the parent that they wanted more from. It can get weird. It helps to remember that you are being treated as the major authority figure in this person's life and not as yourself. It's nothing personal. If someone underestimates you, they're probably underestimating their mother or father. If someone lies to you, it's just what they did around authority figures in the past. In other words, everyone has "an authority problem," and you get to be the authority figure for dozens or hundreds of people.

Here's another way to explain the scenario. When people are giving as much as filmmaking demands, they're in a vulnerable position. Even if they know their jobs well, every film forces them to learn more. As the director, you're in the teacher position. Imagine if your math teacher had a breakdown as you were trying to learn algebra. It would have made learning about parabolas seem all the more impossible.

The cast and crew need someone to count on. Worrying about you makes their job that much more difficult. Worrying about whether you'll ever pull yourself together enough to appreciate them makes their work that much more depressing.

No matter how hard you realize the job of director is, everyone else thinks you have the best deal. In some very real ways, they're right. If the film is any kind of success, you'll get the credit. If the screenwriter did a terrific job, somehow you'll still get the credit for the great story. It's not fair. The opposite is true, too, and also works against the crew. If you do a not-so-great job, no one looks good.

If you're choosing to be a director, chances are it's because you like—or indeed, need—to be in control. When you're the cine-matographer, production designer, actor, etc., someone else is in charge. As much as the weight of responsibility can drive you nuts, you have to remember that it's what you wanted.

Power is a contract. By signing on, cast and crew are agreeing to be led. They're giving you the power to lead them. Your job is to accept and assume it. With all its side effects and responsibilities.

▶▶ 124. WHAT SEPARATES THE DIRECTORS FROM THE DIRECTORS.

Everyone has a way to get what he wants. Babies pick up on crying. Some older kids move on to bullying; some others cultivate being really, really nice. You've developed your own style of persuasion that works for you. The tough part is when it doesn't and you have to find tactics outside your usual vocabulary.

Camille had a directing teacher who regularly fell asleep in (the very small, seminar-style) class—and that was on days he was there. He did say one thing that truly helped, though. Camille faced fir-ing a crew member who was a self-appointed rotten apple. It would have been the first person she had ever fired, and she was scared. "This is what separates the directors from the directors," the teacher said. Giving directions (the root of the term "director") is easy, he said. It's what you do when people won't follow your directions that's the challenge.

In addition to the conflict and the prospect of failure, what's really hard is shifting to a new style of asking for what you want. But you must, because the person you're having the conflict with is asking you to.

While most people respond to patient encouragement, some

are wary of positive reinforcement and only believe you're paying attention when you're yelling. If whatever's natural for you isn't working, then it's not natural for the person on the other side.

In the case of the crew member in question, Camille thought she had tried everything. For her, firing meant saying good-bye. Turns out it was just the trick to get the guy back on track. He needed some negative reinforcement. Once he got it, he was fine. Being a director does not mean you get carte blanche to be yourself. The management part of the job means you have to practice using the sides of yourself you don't normally use.

▶▶ 125. IT'S BETTER TO FIRE THAN BE BURNED.

We've heard of producers who fire someone on the first day (whether or not they deserve it) by way of showing who's in charge. We're not in favor of being this extreme. To us, firing someone in order to assert power reveals a fundamental lack of power.

Still, if someone acts in a way that undermines your authority, you send the wrong message if you don't react. If you accept mistreatment, you give the message that you expect it to happen again. And it will. Both at the hands of the first perpetrator, then on down through the other would-be roosters in the pecking order. The aggression will be aimed at you and anyone else who doesn't resist it.

Accept mistreatment and you send a dangerous message to both the strong and the weak on your cast and crew. Bullies will take the cue and wreak more irritation on you and others. The meek will feel they have no one to protect them. Meanwhile, those with stronger self-esteem will wonder if they've found themselves the proper company.

19

SEX, LIES, AND 16MM

▶▶126. DON'T FALL IN LOVE WITH CAST OR CREW.

It's the emotional equivalent of falling in love at a car-wreck.

High-stakes situations bring out intense dynamics of need and rescue sometimes thought of as romantic. This is the stuff of love stories in 1970s disaster movies, where the heiress falls in love with the plumber, the movie star with the escaped con. What happens afterward? There's a reason why the movies don't ever show that part.

But you're not looking for advice on what makes love last. You just want someone to go home with.

Besides, you say, it's no one's business.

But it is. Since a crew inevitably develops the dynamics of a family, this affair will have the lingering taint of incest. It'll creep people out and eventually will make you feel weird, too.

On the other hand, if the crew hasn't yet achieved these kinds of familial bonds, this kind of thing ensures they won't. Not with you, anyway. You and the partner will have taken your two corps out of the esprit. You'll be treating someone differently from everyone else. Even if it's not a way anyone else wants to be treated by you, it still makes them feel other-ed. If indeed there is jealousy, part of the wrath and mean talk will fall on your chosen partner. Which may cause you pain, anger, and distress, and, in any case, further distract you from the job at hand.

So, you'll just hide the affair.

You can't. Even if you arrive in separate cars, etc., people will know. They'll know even before you two do. You're communicating something more basic, something animals and crew members can smell.

So, who cares what people think?

You do. Having an intimate relationship with someone means sharing some part of yourself that others don't see. Expose yourself this nakedly—even to just one person—and you've exposed yourself to paranoia. What do people know about us? What do they think? What have they heard? What have they said? Who told that lie? Who told that other lie?

So, you've promised each other not to talk about it.

Did *you* keep your promise?

▶▶127. SINCE YOU'LL PROBABLY DO IT ANYWAY, TRY NOT TO SLEEP WITH THEM UNTIL AFTER THE SHOOT.

Remember the classic advice to keep you from getting nervous in front of a group, the thing about seeing everyone in their underwear? Now you're in your underwear, and everyone—the very cast and crew that are supposed to follow your lead—is laughing.

Your partner's also standing around in underwear, being laughed at. Wouldn't he rather be on the other side of the joke? Watch how quickly he can switch sides.

Now you're being laughed at by someone who's actually seen your underwear. As if you didn't have enough problems.

▶▶128. SINCE YOU'LL PROBABLY SLEEP WITH THEM ANYWAY, TRY TO CHOOSE SOMEONE WHO CAN'T RUIN THE FILM.

Sleep with a crew member and she can still be expected to do her job. Sleep with one of the actors, though, and your authority is totally shot. Remember the thing about actors playing out the part of children, with directors taking over the functions of parent. How, short of some incestuous dynamic, are you going to make this work at all?

Also, consider this: you have good nights, you have bad nights.

The morning after good nights, the actor's going to be more in *that* mood than any other. Maybe it can work for the scene. As long as it's a romance, and as long as they can channel all that stuff in the direction of their fellow actor. Jesus, what if they can?

The morning after bad nights, you may have trouble maintaining eye contact, let alone directing him in a scene. Is he angry? Maybe that can work for the scene. But what if it's a romance and he kisses that other actor with so much more conviction than what you got last night?

▸▸ 129. SINCE YOU'LL BREAK UP ANYWAY, TRY TO DO IT AFTER PRINCIPAL PHOTOGRAPHY.

Usually, it's not "if this relationship ends." It's when. When that time comes, you'll understand the claim that it's a thin line between love and hate. Whatever you had (passion, loyalty, honesty) gets turned inside out and turned against you and your film.

An ex-lover becomes a D.P. who drops the camera. A sound guy who forgets to press "record." An editor who loses trims. A producer who sends the tape to Sundance a day after the deadline. On purpose.

To do good work, people need to give their whole heart to something. If it's broken, there's less of it they can give.

Even if she goes quietly, what do you expect the crew to say? Did you book and train a replacement before you broke up? Is the crew happy to work with someone new at the eleventh hour, or to pick up the slack of someone else's old job?

All this is assuming *you* did the breaking up. What if it was the other way around? How's your mood going to help you pull off a comedy—romantic or otherwise? Are you ready to fire someone just because she doesn't want to sleep with you anymore? Isn't that sexual harassment?

The ex-crew-member-lover is a dangerous enemy to have. He not only has the impetus to criticize how good (or bad) a director you were, but he has the temptation to gossip about how "good" you were (or weren't) in all those other ways . . .

▸▸130. IF YOU STILL HAVE A PERSONAL LIFE, DON'T INVITE IT ONTO THE SET.

Your crew is giving you more of their attention, creativity, and patience than your main squeeze has given you since your third date. They want and need to be recognized and appreciated for it. This doesn't mean they're waiting or wanting to be kissed. But they are expecting a kind of loyalty, intimacy, and attention to what's important here—namely, the film, and not your date on Friday night. Don't two-time them by bringing your extra-romantic interests onto your set.

Bringing your boyfriend or girlfriend to the set is a kind of taunt, similar to cruel kids' "I've got the ice cream, and you don't get any" chant. Kids will tell you that it's not fair. It's not. It's also demoralizing. Don't give yourself special treatment. You don't deserve it. At least, not more than everyone else. If your personal life comes onto the set anyway, have them bring enough cupcakes for everyone.

20

DON'T MAKE THINGS MORE DIFFICULT THAN THEY ARE

▸▸131. THE STRAIGHTEST LINE BETWEEN TWO POINTS.

We live impressed by the road less traveled. By making a film, you're already taking it. Now that you've made your big statement, consider accepting some ordinary common sense and don't let yourself get tangled in all the potential solutions to a problem. All things being equal, the simplest solution is the best.

Once upon a time there was a knot no one could untie . . . A peasant named Gordius created it to attach an ox yoke to his cart. Legend said that whoever loosened the knot would become ruler of all Asia. Many failed. Then one day in 333 B.C., Alexander the Great rode by. He stopped and looked at the knot. After a moment he took out his sword. With one slash the knot was history and he went on to rule Asia.

A short solution is as good as a long one. Seven hundred years ago an English monk, philosopher, and theologian named Occam put it this way: "What can be done with fewer assumptions is done in vain with more." His theory, known as Occam's Razor, asserts that when two theories work equally well, choose the simpler one.

Instead of living by the Occam philosophy, many filmmakers seem to be adherents to a more hermeneutic worldview, which advocates taking circular paths toward an eventual discovery of a solution at the center. Alexander didn't conquer the world with hermeneutics. The shortest distance between two points is a straight line.

▸▸132. IF YOU CAN'T BE WITH THE SHOT YOU WANT, LOVE THE SHOT YOU'RE WITH.

The audience knows nothing about, and could care even less about, how you had originally planned the shot. Maybe that special shot was an artful way of delivering this scene. But who has time for art at the point when you are losing light and you are about to be kicked out of your location? You need to tell the story, fast.

Ask yourself, what is the one thing that needs to happen in this scene so that the story can move on to the next one, and the one after that? Boil it down to one critical thing that must happen in this scene and no other: the gesture, the word, the ultimatum, the introduction of a prop, the single raised eyebrow that lets us know the character is suspicious, etc.

Shoot it and move on.

▸▸133. AVOID EXISTENTIAL CRISIS, GET THE CUTAWAYS.

Cutaways mean you have options to tell the story you set out to film versus being at the mercy of creating a "story" out of whatever shots don't have a boom pole in them. Without a cutaway, an unusable shot is unusable no matter which way you slice it, because you have nothing to slice it with. Building cutaways into your shot list means that you can use the good parts of otherwise fundamentally flawed shots.

Now you can use the shot up to where the actor inappropriately breaks out laughing, go to the cutaway, and come back once the actor's finished laughing and the boom mike that he's laughing about has finally cleared the shot.

If you have only one shot of a piece of action, that's all you have. If you have another shot of that action, from a clearly distinct angle (think thirty degrees or more including top down or bottom up or a vastly different frame—such as from close up to long shot), suddenly you have something to cut away to, and back from.

Meaning you've much more than doubled the potential usefulness of the first shot. Because now you can cut away and back to it as many times as you want. With a third shot, mathematically you've increased the possibilities by some even bigger number we don't know how to calculate.

▸▸134. JUST SAY NO TO DOLLY SHOTS, JIB ARMS, CRANES, AND CHERRY PICKERS.

The problem with trick shots is that they demand to be arias, standing alone and sometimes apart from the rest of the film. These gadgets introduce a style and pacing of camera movement that is unique to them and may stand out within the context of the film.

Shots rarely have the luxury of existing on their own. A basic principle of editing is to cut to a shot only if it has as much or more energy as the previous one does. This keeps the film moving forward. Cutting from a moving dolly shot to a still cutaway means breaking this rule every time. Editing dolly-move shots together? Now you've got the problem of consistent pacing. Without the same rhythm, you're cutting together the equivalent of a bad dance scene where someone's always stepping on someone else's toes.

The pace of the camera move can also be at odds with the pace of the action within the shot. The problem is, you can't change the pace of shots in which the movement is not only inside the frame but in the camera move itself. You won't know the pace your film needs, scene to scene and within scenes, until you edit it. The wrong timing on trick shots means they can stop a scene cold. If it's your only shot covering the action, you and your editor are at its mercy.

These editing hassles compound the time you'll have already wasted negotiating with the special equipment on the set. At the beginner's level, these gadgets are telltale giveaways that someone on the crew (D.P., director, or producer) didn't want to feel like a beginner. They rented the remote-controlled helicopter cam to impress themselves.

The cast and crew pay for this insecurity. The machines unfairly command their time and energy. Simple actions get the production anxiety of Busby Berkeley numbers. Actors will resent the effort you put into making their work sync up to the machine rather than the other way around. ("No, cross in front of the camera when the camera is right here . . . not there . . .") They'll legitimately feel you've put the cart before the horse.

▸▸135. ACCEPT THE SCRIPT SUPERVISOR INTO YOUR LIFE.

Script supervisors take intensive courses, and working on your film can provide a welcome "internship" (read: unpaid) opportunity. Lucky you. Script supervisors are incredibly patient, work the longest hours, and never take a break. They're focused, even-tempered, concentrated, and, along with the sound guys, the nicest and most modest people on your set. None of which means that you should ignore them.

Think you know better than they do what the actor should do in the retake? It's all in the details. Just how observant are you?

- What did you have for breakfast this morning?
- Did you pour the cereal or the milk in first?
- Was your shirt tucked in or not? On what side?
- How much growth was on your chin?
- What time was it on your watch?
- What section of the newspaper did you read first?
- At which point, exactly, did you touch your hair?
- Was the glass half full, half empty, or neither?

This was your breakfast. The thing you do every day, sort of. You failed to recall it in ways that would matter if it was a scene in a film. The script supervisor—God knows how—would have gotten everything down. Your performance at breakfast was undoubtedly very natural the first time. But what if you had to do a second take?

Maintaining continuity from take to take and with your coverage will allow your editor to use shots without having to worry about irregularities in the action, wardrobe, or props. It means your editor won't have to throw out a perfectly good close-up because it doesn't match the master in an obvious way. Given that you are shooting out of sequence ninety-nine percent of the time, the script supervisor maintains the only link to the film's temporal and visual continuity. He or she will help you remember what the actor's hair looked like *exactly* when you shot the first half of this scene three weeks ago. And as ridiculous as it sounds—you should care.

▶▶136. IF YOU BINGE ON VISA, SAVE ROOM FOR THE MONTHLY PAYMENTS.

Money costs money. Since you don't have enough of it in the first place, you can't afford to be credit illiterate and spend too much of it on interest.

Approach money, and credit, seriously. Which doesn't mean taking any of it personally. You are not your debt. Your net worth is no indication of your true worth. There is nothing immoral about being poor. And in America there is nothing wrong with being in debt. Just do it carefully. Well-managed debt pays off in greater lines of credit at lower rates.

David Davidson, self-supporting independent filmmaker, is a master of credit card use, orchestrating up to eighteen at a time to finance his productions. Here are his tips for using credit cards before they use you:

1. Never charge more than you think you can pay back in two years. Anything more than that will leave you feeling crippled and under an immovable mountain.

2. Pay at least your minimum monthly payment the day the bill comes in. This way there will be no chance of your being late. Credit card companies don't send you your bill more than an average of ten to twelve days before it's due.

Don't forget that they charge late fees and jack up your interest rate, too. Lateness will jeopardize your chances of getting the super-low interest rate cards that a well-run, sustainable credit card lifestyle depends on.

3. One trick to not ever being late is to link cards to your checking account, authorizing them to automatically withdraw minimum monthly payments. Not all credit card companies offer this option, though. Perhaps they want you to fall into a stupor and collect late fees from you. In this case, set up preposted envelopes on a highly visible wall, and also key a reminder function into a computer datebook so that you can be reminded by electric shock.

4. Rotate balances to lower interest rates with regularity. Create a calendar that will alert you as to the days when your trial low-interest periods will be over.

5. Stagger your low-interest credit card applications to coincide with when you will need them. If you don't then you might run out of your low-interest periods before you really need them. Don't apply for all the low-interest cards at once, or all your low-interest opportunities will expire at the same time.

6. Get a copy of your credit report regularly and scan it for any negative ratings or reports. Protest them all in writing. You can get a free copy of your report once a year by writing to TRW.

7. How you manage student loans and car loan debt matters. Do it well, and credit card companies will respond with interest.

8. Don't apply for new cards unless your credit is in reasonably good shape. Rejections from card companies show up as negative ratings on your report and make other card companies less likely to take you on as a risk.

9. If you are in a high-risk index on your report, consider working with a lawyer that specializes in repairing credit. The money you spend getting your credit fixed will be made up over the time you spend paying lower interest rates on your borrowed money. Beware of schemes marketed in mailers, on the Internet, and on chain-link fences by freeways that pitch instant credit repair. Oftentimes these involve getting new Social Security numbers and changing your name. This can amount to a felony if debtors can prove that your reason for doing it is to escape financial responsibility.

10. Save room for your monthly payments. It is highly inadvisable to use those credit card checks to pay bills because this money will be considered a cash advance and will be charged at the highest, more usurious interest rate allowed by law. However, when you are living on the edge and credit is financing your life, then be sure to leave some room on the cards. In a pinch, you'll have to use one to make a payment on another card. It's much better to incur the high-interest hit than it is to take a credit-rating bruise for being late.

11. For every card you have, pick a partner card which will be the rescue card in case you are unable to make the monthly payments on the first. On the first card, figure out the minimum monthly payment if you charge the card to the max of your current limit. That's the money you're going to have to come up with to bail that card out. On the other card, figure out how much room you need to save in order to be able to make those payments, for as long as you think you'll need to. This is a do-it-yourself credit insurance system. Your credit report will thank you.

12. Assertively seek out better rates. Call to ask for an extension on the promotional rate or to ask if they have any promo-

tional rate reductions you may not know about. This often does work.

13. Play Peter against Paul. Call credit card companies to let them know you'll be closing the account if they don't match another company's better offer. If a lender can see that you have a lot of expenses locked up on other cards, you can talk them into consolidating your debt at a negotiated low APR. They'll work with you, especially if you are never late on payments and keep a balance (larger is in most cases better).

14. Listen to the Treasury secretary, not only for his vague Horace-like economic metaphors, but because when the government jacks up interest rates, you know who else will, too.

15. Subscribe to several credit web pages to get e-mail notification on low-rate cards. Apply online, speeding the usually sluggish world of bank-to-bank transfers.

16. Do balance transfers over the phone. Don't use checks because they can take too long to arrive, and to credit to the new card company's account. No transfers are instant. Call the payment in several days early to accommodate the Pony Express mentality that can leave you in limbo between two cards.

If you're planning on using credit cards as the primary source of your film's funding, credit card guru Dave has this additional advice:

1. At least two months before production, apply like crazy for the cards. Perhaps eight to ten of them. On one or two cards, put the producer and the production designer's name so they can use them when convenience is necessary. Forget the D.P.

and other department heads, as production will handle most of their transactions.

2. With these applications processing, other card-offering companies will perk up and send additional applications. If you apply, receive, and let the cards sit, the effect is like bait to other companies.

3. Paying cards off regularly and aggressively attracts credit card applications. Having a balance and diligently knocking it down sends up the fiscal flare. An entirely unsolicited forty-plus applications, convenience checks, and notifications literally broke Dave's mailbox.

4. Credit cards are useful not just for the credit line but for the programmed, automatic ceiling for charges. If others are going to be using your cards during production, you could call the companies to preset lower denial ceilings as a safeguard.

5. Track all cards on a spreadsheet. Keep statistics regarding what the transaction was for, the date, which card, the authorization number, the promotional interest rate, and when the rate will change to a higher APR. Also track credit-per-card remaining and total credit remaining. Managing multiple streams of credit isn't easy, but most of the debt-payment management can be planned well before and after production. Not during. During the hurricane, no one can be trusted to remember to pay debts. Everyone's too busy watching the furniture fly around.

6. Separate the cards you use for film and professional needs from the ones you use for personal needs. This will help you monitor and keep track of your spending and will be an aid at tax time when the goal is to spot and deduct all qualified business expenses.

7. Only use your cards to pay for budgeted items in whatever sphere: personal or film. Having budgets in these areas is a must before you put your cards to use. Psychologically, it is key to know that what you spent the credit on has gone toward bringing you closer to your goals. Without this rational base it is likely that a credit card lifestyle will allow you to get trapped in a cycle of emotional, compulsive spending that will lead you to financial ruin. Spending from pre-ordained budgets will allow you to plan and will remove the guilt and exhilaration cycles you could otherwise drown in.

21

LOCATION, LOCATION, AND LOCATION

▶▶137. DADA DRIVING AND LOCATION SCOUTING.

You should always be location scouting. For the film you're making now, the one your friend is making, the one you'll make next, or the one you can make now that you've discovered the location.

Getting the location can be the biggest hurdle and nerve-wracking hassle of no-budget filmmaking. When you can't pay, it's hard to ask people to vacate their home, risk damage to their furniture, shut down their restaurant, etc. Which is why it makes sense, for your next film, to go about it "backward." Discover a location that inspires you, secure it, then write the film you see there. This is what Larry Meistrich and Nick Gomez did on *Laws of Gravity*. They wrote the script and made the film in the loft they already had a lease on. Indeed, to finance the other stuff (camera, film, etc.), they rented the loft out to other film crews, and used it for script readings that somehow also provided a revenue stream.

Drive aimlessly. Take the opportunity when stopped at lights to look around. Visit the places that catch your eye. Talk to the owner or manager. Tell them that you literally pulled over because the place was so great and inspiring. It will be true and sincere. Let them share their own enthusiasm for their place with you. Let them tell you its history, what they find particularly interesting and wonderful about it. Share this pleasure and respect with them. When they ask what you do, answer, "Filmmaker," but make no overt reference to their place as the location of your next film. Let them come up with the brilliant idea.

If the idea doesn't come to them, let yourself imagine out loud. "Gosh, I could really imagine a great action scene here. It gives me ideas for a film." Leave them with the idea (indeed, it's true) that their location has literally inspired a story. Say good-bye with the promise, "So, if I do write that thriller, I'll come back and see you." If you've gotten this far, it has something to do with the fact that they like and trust you. Enough to remember you when you show up later with your producer in tow and a location release in hand.

People are a lot easier to get to know when you don't need anything from them—at least, not right then. So lay your tracks in advance.

▸▸ 138. CHOOSE A LOCATION YOU CAN DRIVE BACK FROM WITH YOUR EYES CLOSED.

Tiare's last film at AFI involved shooting in a little town in a little patch of desert gloriously billed by location scouts as "the middle of nowhere."

The location fit the story's needs perfectly, but by day two of production, this seemed like small compensation. The town was four and a half hours away from L.A. and an hour from the nearest grocery store. Cast and crew were forced to sleep at the location, a generally uninhabited fifties-era motel, with dubiously washed linens, an intermittently effective swamp cooler filtering the desert summer's heat, and a profusion of flying cockroaches and burrowing tarantulas in residence.

Because the nearest alternative to Jim the motel keeper's food was the "hot serve" nachos at the Texaco station a half hour away, cast and crew were held hostage to his cooking. Needless to say, it was terrible. But the mystery meat sure as hell didn't taste any better when they learned that the town's entire population belonged to a coven of satanic worshipers. Led by Jim.

Because there was a profound lack of access to even the basic conveniences, not to mention those basic to film production, everything had to be imported. If something was forgotten, it was forgone. If someone brought the wrong (neon orange) curtains, the wrong neon orange curtains went up. Equipment that was broken stayed broken. The associate producer, who might have signed on to the crew with some dreams of doing some "creative producing" spent the entire shoot making emergency runs to L.A.

When, after numerous long days and nights of shooting, the location finally wrapped, the actors were exhausted and eager to get home. An equally tired P.A. offered to drive them back to L.A. What you think happens next did: he rolled his soft-top Jeep off the road, throwing passengers out of the car. The only good news is that no one was permanently hurt.

Think of what you have to gain by staying close to the comforts and conveniences of home. If this cautionary tale isn't enough, here are some more incentives:

SAG contracts delineate a "studio zone" beyond which New York- and L.A.-based actors are to be paid an extra per diem. Its purpose is to ensure that members aren't schlepping farther than necessary without compensation for the inconvenience. In L.A. the studio zone is the circle defined by a thirty-mile radius from the Beverly Center—a mall (it's L.A.). If you're working with SAG actors under an agreement in which their pay is deferred, if your movie ever makes any money, you'll not only be responsible for paying their salaries but the per diems they accrued while working on your film.

Insurance often doesn't cover location shooting outside a given area (our schools' insurance was limited to the studio zone, for example). You don't want to find this out when you need it, although we're not sure exposure to satanic worship is covered anywhere anyway.

▶▶139. WHY SCHLEP TO TEN LOCATIONS WHEN ONE WILL DO JUST FINE?

"Company move" are two words that don't go great together. It's like packing up a thirty-person family and transferring them plus their luggage from Kennedy Airport to Newark International on a hot day with a plane to catch. "Camera? I thought *you* had the camera."

Cluster your locations—keep them as close to walking distance as possible. A great location is one that can be used for a variety of shots, doubling as an entirely different place if necessary.

Your actors can do the same good job in front of the white wall in your apartment as they can in front of the pink wall across town. If you're in love with the pink, paint your apartment. Use close-ups for one of the best reasons they were invented: faking a location. A wall is a wall is a wall. If your desired location had a great paneled oak wall, you can go out and buy yourself some great fake oak paneling and prop it up behind where your actors will sit.

If you're still caught between whining and despair about being anchored to a single location, your imagination is failing you. If pink paint and oak paneling don't solve your problem, use your pen and rewrite. Don't forget that studio lots were built on the real efficiencies of shooting in one place.

▶▶140. YOUR OWN BACK LOT.

If you're at school, or a friend is, think of the campus as your own back lot. Outside production companies pay by the thousands to shoot at locations you can use for free. Productions shot at USC and AFI, including *The Graduate* (USC doubled for U.C. Berkeley), *The Big Picture* (AFI), and *Forrest Gump* (scenes shot at USC) served as good reminders to look in our backyard.

Advantages include:

- Locations are free, and often there's plenty of architectural diversity.
- Utilities are free.
- Locations are automatically covered by the school's insurance.
- Street scenes can be faked, with traffic totally controlled.

- You can use the school's dollies and trucks to wheel stuff between sets.
- Part of your crew can prepare the next shot at the math building while you're working on your shot in front of the biology lab.
- The cafeteria is nearby and the food is cheap (especially if students on your crew already have meal plans).
- Crew members can run back to their rooms for stuff.
- You don't have to pay for security.
- You can confirm the availability and safety of power sources with a campus electrician before you start filming.
- There's someone to call if the power shuts down.
- Your student crew already knows where everything is.
- You can work with the school to book space on campus to store your props.
- The school newspaper's photographer can take production photos for free.
- It's easy to return your equipment to the school's loading dock on time—just push the dolly.
- If there is a theater department, they might have props, wardrobe, and flats you can borrow or have customized.

The advantages of such subsidized conveniences are so great that you should consider becoming a student just for the benefits. For a $50 investment you can enroll full-time at a community college in *any* program (not just film). The ID card can help you score discounts at prop and equipment houses, as well as on film stock. If you don't mind failing your classes, you can get all the advantages of school without any of the homework.

▶▶141. THE WEATHER DOESN'T TAKE VISA.

Plan to shoot the location exteriors first, but book an indoor location for these same days. If it rains, you've got a place to shoot other scenes so you don't fall behind schedule. By scheduling the exterior locations up front, you've got some room in your schedule to wait for the weather to clear.

If it looks like weather's going to be a problem, rewrite whatever important scenes were to take place outside and set them indoors. You can just send a camera person out to catch an establishing shot at any point later when the clouds finally break.

On the other hand, some productions pay a lot of money to simulate rain. If you've got it and you can make it work for that scene, use it. It'll look . . . real. As if Mother Nature takes your calls.

▶▶142. LANDLORDS LEARN FROM THEIR MISTAKES. GET THE LOCATION SHOTS THE FIRST TIME.

Maybe they're happy to let their house be in pictures, until you start scratching the floors, stomping on the flower beds, using foul language in front of their kids, and making clear that you lied about how long it was going to take.

Crews are high-impact and all too often arrogant, treating locations like they are a means to making a film and not someone's home.

While fully expecting something to go wrong anyway, train and plead with your crew to do the following:

1. No smoking, especially indoors.

2. If smoking's a matter of life or death, use an ashtray or a soda can; don't try to hide the butts.

3. No food or drink indoors. Especially drinks, which will spill, putting furniture, equipment, and electrical safety at risk.

4. Check out the electrical capacities beforehand, and if in doubt over whether the system can take the load, use a generator or don't use the place.

5. Assign one person to be "bad cop" assigned to do nothing but protect the place. On bigger shoots this is the location manager.

6. Bring your own toilet paper.

7. No messing around with the owner's personal things. One crew actually read Camille's journals to kill time, which was the last time she let her apartment be used for other people's shoots.

8. Bring your own towels, etc., for removing makeup.

9. Put mats down everywhere before anyone walks in.

10. Don't allow anyone to drag any piece of equipment or prop. Lifting saves the floor.

11. No using or visiting any room that's not currently in use.

12. No mean comments about any aspect of the person's home or decorating style. Flattery only.

13. No stepping on or around anything that seems like it might have been planted on purpose by a landscaper.

14. No standing on furniture to get to other stuff.

15. No free-style redecorating without the most explicit permission. No moving of anything without drawing an explicit diagram or taking Polaroids showing how it's supposed to go back.

16. Use your own cell phones, even if it costs more than using their phone.

17. No complaining that the owner has to use THEIR OWN PLACE for anything: planned or unplanned.

18. Overestimate, by double, how long the whole thing will take. Negotiate for that amount of time. You will need it.

19. Don't do anything that could upset the neighbors, because they'll blame the owners for trusting you.

▸▸143. YOUR APARTMENT IS READY FOR ITS CLOSE-UP.

You lost your location. Even if you found a new location today, you'd have to get a permit, which generally requires three days in L.A., and anywhere between one day and one week in N.Y. depending on the scale and complexity of your production.

If your backup location is your apartment, you still need a permit. Unless you own the building or house you live in, you will need your landlord's signature on the permit application. To avoid delays when you can least spare them, we recommend getting a permit for your apartment before production starts for the entire conceivable run of your shoot. Then you have a legitimate and ready backup should disaster, in its many possible forms, strike.

There's a good reason to file for permits, in addition to the fact that they're required by law. Doing so automatically alerts police and fire departments that you're filming. In case someone calls to complain during your shoot, you can't be shut down—at least not automatically.

If you have any scenes with violence and/or guns, you better take your permits very seriously. If the police confuse your prop guns with real ones (not knowing that you're making a film), you could get very hurt. USC students shooting without a permit found themselves surrounded by helicopters and a SWAT team responding to an alert that there were "gunmen" on the roof of the school's parking lot. Don't risk getting caught in the cross fire of confusion. Get the permit. Permits are free for students, so if you are one, money is no excuse not to have one.

Here's the question everyone asks: if a film shoots in your apartment and no one hears it, does it really need a permit? No, but there is a lot riding on that "if." All a cop has to see is a grip truck with people sitting on the lift gate smoking and extension cords running inside to figure out that a film is happening. The cop doesn't even have to be driving by; a neighbor could call the police, upset about any number of inconveniences, real or imagined, including that he couldn't find a parking space on the block because of all your crew's vehicles.

When the cop shows up calmly asking for your permit, you want to be able to very calmly show him one and continue shooting. Any other response and you'll be shut down.

22

THE LOST, THE STOLEN,
AND THE BROKEN

▶▶ 144. BE INSURED AND BE SANE.

Many property owners won't even let you in the door to ask if you can use a location unless you have insurance. In New York insurance is never optional since you need it in order to get a permit to shoot anything, anywhere.

Accidents always happen on film sets, and locations usually take a beating. Because you can't claim to know what anything (that doesn't belong to you) is really worth, without insurance you'll be stuck paying the highest possible replacement cost. The sky might suddenly become the limit. Insurance companies, on the other hand, have departments of people who evaluate claims and decide what constitutes fair reimbursement.

Insurance protects not only whatever passes as your bank account, but also the relationships involved in making your film. Not only between you and the property owner, but between you and whoever dropped the camera. It's easier to work things out if you're facing a reasonable deductible versus the full cost of a $25,000 camera.

▸▸145. DON'T BORROW ANYTHING
YOU CAN'T REPLACE.

Dear Luis,

I'm writing to say how sorry I am that we never found your vintage Mexican baseball pennants. The ones you had in your room growing up. The ones we used on the set in the little boy's bedroom in "Carnaval," the first film you directed at AFI. The one in which I was your production designer. I know the pennants had tremendous sentimental as well as collectible value.

After the shoot, when all the rented and borrowed props were returned, your pennants were simply nowhere to be found. I promise you that I looked high and low. In every corner of the location, and in all the more improbable places, including my car, Michael's car, and just about everyone else's car. I went back to the location months later with the hope that perhaps they were on that out-of-reach shelf in a corner in the room. No luck. I have just not been able to accept that they were stolen. I continue to search for them even now.

Luis, every time I see you, I still feel the pain of responsibility for the loss of those pennants. If I had stopped to think about how irreplaceable they were, I would have done the right thing: asked you to just put them back in your car where they would have been safe.

Luis, I'm sorry. I hope you can forgive, if not forget. I know it does not help you that I have not lost a prop since. I still hold on to hope that they'll turn up.

Sincerely,
Tiare

23

HOW I LEARNED TO STOP WORRYING AND LOVE THE SOUND

▶▶146. SOUND WILL SAVE YOUR FILM.

Discovering sound—its complete centrality to the emotional power of your film—is the major revelation that comes only after people make their first film. People think that image in film is everything.

We discover enlightenment the hard way, by noticing how bad sound irretrievably destroys our films. Without sound it is next to impossible to watch films as "film"—or anything more than a slide show. With bad sound—indecipherable dialogue, rocky changes in sound balance, sudden gaps of existential nothing, out-of-sync words and effects—films can literally make an audience nauseous.

While a blurry image has the opportunity nowadays to seem intentional, bad sound does not get excused. It's too hard to. Incomprehensible sound is .... incomprehensible. Whereas film images are shown at a staccato twenty-four frames per second, for which the eye adjusts, sound is recorded and broadcast as a continuous band. Interruptions to it are jarring on the most basic level. They are enough not only to throw an audience out of the film, but catapult them out of the theater.

Bad or even mediocre sound is all the more regrettable when you consider what an awesome, spectacularly powerful, hypnotic tool it is.

Sound is . . .

- the door to the audience's unconscious. The stealthy way in which you create a safe, seductive, complete environment in which the audience can let go, and experience both sound and picture.
- the space and landscape of the film. What makes the 2-D space of film imagery transform into 3-D experience. Indeed, if you count emotion, a 4-D experience.
- the one continuous through-line of the film and, as such, the film's foundation, authority, and lifeline.
- what tells an audience what to feel. Whether it's romance, or comedy, drama or horror, or any combination of these. It cues you when to laugh and when to cry.

Sound can . . .

- make the audience think and feel things are happening when they're not.
- suggest a much scarier monster than one you can create in pictures. The shark in *Jaws* is scarier when it's not on screen, but rather when it stalks unseen, represented only by its menacing theme.
- bridge your film's unmatched shots. Slice two discontinuous images together but keep the sound constant and rich. The audience will feel like they're still in the same space.
- distract from a missed shot or a bad performance.
- eliminate the need for expensive special effects (as in: "show" the train wreck offscreen, with a sound fx).

Sound editing is the one stage of filmmaking that doesn't require you to make all your decisions once or forever hold your peace. Unlike picture editing, which is designed to narrow possibilities, sound editing is a cumulative and additive process, meant to add to your options up until and through the mix. Gather sounds and enjoy the luxury of watching them against the film in any combination until you have what you want.

Film is the art of picture *and* sound. These are the 1 + 1 that, added together, equal more than 2. Together, and only together, they make a film. Without good sound you're sacrificing your film's potential or even your film, period.

▶▶147. A FEW WORDS ON VOICE-OVER.

Voice-over gets the wrong reputation as a cop-out. It is when it is, and isn't when it's not. It's OK to use voice-over if the film can work without it.

Voice-over can reveal a secret side of one of the characters, or add an entirely new, and perhaps never seen, character to your cast. You can use it like a two-way mirror, provoking a separate truth, one that renders the voices of the other characters unreliable. The unknown authority has more authority than the visible one. In the movies, God always speaks in voice-over.

Terrence Malick's three films are enough to prove the artistic legitimacy, not to mention possibilities, of voice-over. In *Days of Heaven*, a little girl with an unnaturally aged voice tells the story of her makeshift family, telegraphing an aura of doomed possibility from the film's beginning. In *Badlands*, Sissy Spacek's deadpan voice adds another layer of strange danger to the violence of her new man. In *The Thin Red Line*, soldiers' inner voices map the shadows of their lives and deaths, giving an ebbing echo of their souls.

Voice-over is intimate, like a letter written to just one person. It gives an audience the unequaled pleasure of eavesdropping. It can give your film a haunted quality or, used in a different sort of counterpoint, add to its humor.

▶▶148. MUSIC, THE HARD WAY.

What looks like the easiest thing in the world—using a piece of prerecorded music in your film's soundtrack—is actually quite time-consuming.

With prerecorded music you'll need to get *all* of the following rights, often from different parties:

- Lyrics: These are called publishing rights, and are held by companies or individuals. You can get information on who owns what by calling the New York or L.A. offices of the American Society of Composers and Performers (ASCAP) and Broadcast Music, Inc. (BMI)—two clearinghouses with this information.
- Composition: These rights may belong to someone else than the rights to the lyrics do. Track down who through ASCAP or BMI.
- Recording, or "sync" (for "synchronization"), rights: Someone owns the rights to the specific recording you're listening to. This can be someone different from the one(s) who owns the rights to the lyrics and composition. Contact the rights department of the recording company listed on the label of your CD or cassette.
- Performance: Singers and musicians retain the right to their own performance on the recording. If the recording label's rights department is not in the position to license these to you, you'll need to get leads by tracking down EACH of the performers to get their written permission.

Even if you're doing your own recording of a song someone else wrote, while you don't need to get the sync rights or the performance rights (other than permission from the musicians you're working with), you nevertheless still need to clear the rights to the composition and the lyrics.

▸▸149. MUSIC, THE EASY WAYS.

Composers from all over the world are ready to work for free, creating music to which you hold all the rights.

- Universities with music departments have composing students who can see your film as an opportunity to practice. Post an ad there or get in touch with faculty and ask for recommendations.
- Look at other student or independent films, note the composer whose work you liked, and call her.
- Fully cleared music is available for download or purchase online. Just type "royalty free music" into your favorite search engine and revel in the results.
- Put a (free) listing in *Backstage West* or *Dramalogue*, and tapes will come to you.

▸▸ 150. SOUND WILL GIVE YOU ANOTHER REVENUE SOURCE.

The same logic that brought us product placement is making its way to the real estate of your film's soundtrack. The shift from filmmakers paying to use music to being compensated for the gesture is happening gradually. While films still pay a raft of licensors for the right to play a song (hence the two prior sections), some music companies are willing to package and give the music to a film for free as long as they're convinced that it will achieve meaningful distribution (i.e., free advertising for their artists).

You only have negotiating power at the beginning, while your soundtrack is still virgin territory. A record label may be interested only in providing the *entire* music package to your film. Or, without the leverage you can create by bidding two labels against each other, you may manage to get the music for free, but give up any rights to revenue generated by the soundtrack in return. Don't put music in your film with the hope of getting the rights, let alone a profitable deal later. You'll only risk getting sued. Make sure the deal comes before the mix.

On films made by studios, soundtracks can go platinum with the "synergistic" cooperation of the parent company's record labels. On your film, you can think of the soundtrack as one of the ancillary rights you retain. The do-it-yourself power of the digital revolution gives you the chance to start your own record division. Through the Web you can find companies that can, via correspondence, master and press your CD professionally, and even design and print your package art. Then it's up to you to sell it, which you can also do online.

▶▶151. WHY YOU WON'T FIX IT IN THE MIX.

Because sound is among the last stages in the process, and because sound guys (there's really no other shorthand term) tend to be so even-tempered, helpful, and patient, the line "We'll fix it in the mix" gets heard all too often.

It becomes the excuse and rallying cry for mistakes in everyone else's department; while sound can do a lot, there are limits to its capacities to fix, say, the film's color balance. The line also gets overused by directors as they tepidly reassure the mixer that it's a good idea to get this shot now even though a fleet of jets overhead makes the sound totally useless.

You don't want to fix it in the mix. Not only because you can't, but also because you need to keep your sound editors' time focused on the creative possibilities, not the technical harassments, of your film.

In photography, a good negative is one that has enough "information," meaning a full range of recording of the available light. These negatives afford you the possibility of any and all tonal and contrast variations in the print. Likewise, in the case of sound, the cleaner your production sound is, the more you can do with it.

Without background interference married to the sound of your actors' lines, you can re-create or thoroughly invent any environment you want. If, on the other hand, the actor's voice is married to the sound of the plane overhead, you can't do anything about it. You'll need to rerecord.

"We'll do ADR" is the runner-up for overused and foolhardy excuses. Additional Dialogue Recording is expensive, and some actors are better at it than others. It's next to impossible to get the new recording to match the old in terms of microphone angle, distance, and the inevitable ambient sounds that got mixed into the original production sound's recording. For the actors' tones to match, and sound like they are in the same scene, you'll have to get *everyone* who was in the scene to come to the ADR session. This is easier if they're still in town, still remember the character, don't have a cold, and still want to take your calls.

You may have taken so long with picture editing that actors will have resentfully forgotten about your project by the time you call. A USC postproduction record holder had to plead with his lead actor to come in for ADR five years after his shoot. A lot can happen in that time.

To get the sound right the first time, bring the sound guys with you when you've narrowed down locations. Solicit their opinion on the site's acoustical viability, and believe what they tell you. If the place is in the flight plan of an international airport, next to a fire or police station, near a freeway, or above a noisy restaurant, it matters. Go at the time of day or night you intend to shoot and listen for trains, the sound of school getting out, and any other predictable, systemic interruptions. Bad sound conditions are as detrimental to your shoot as bad lighting. The sound guys may not speak as loudly, or insist with the arrogance of a D.P., but they're not lying. If the sound isn't good, you'll pay in the end.

▶▶152. SOUND'S EQUIVALENTS TO SHOOTING WITH THE LENS CAP ON.

Here are the dumb mistakes you may have to make once in order to avoid them forever more:

- Running out of tape in the middle of a take
- Forgetting to press record at the same time as play
- Accidentally taping over the last take that you had gone back to check

- Forgetting to unplug the refrigerator
- Forgetting to plug the refrigerator back in and spoiling the food
- Forgetting to turn off the air conditioning
- Forgetting to insist that everyone turn their cell phones, beepers, and walkie-talkies off before a take, as well as unplugging any phones near the set
- Forgetting to turn the "shooting" light above the stage door on so potential intruders are warned to wait until after the shot is taken before walking in
- Forgetting to turn the "shooting" light above the stage door off and leaving crew stranded outside, debating whether you're still shooting, about to shoot, or just forgot to turn the light off
- Forgetting to tape "room tone" (a minute or two's worth of silence) on location so that you don't have to go back for it
- Forgetting to tape "ambient sound" on location (of people at the market, etc.) so that you don't have to go back to for it
- Leaving the actor's remote mike on even when he takes a rest room break
- Not having an extra battery for the one day of the year when the mike needs it
- Not getting a tail slate at the end of a tail-slated shot (often the camera operator's fault). This leaves you with syncing up the voices or, even worse, the footsteps by hand (a shortcut to insanity)
- Selecting a sound loop for a mix that has an unusual sound (cough, laugh, the beginning of a word in it), which will now surface over and over again in your soundtrack
- Mixing a song you don't have the rights to in the final mix, only to be threatened with a lawsuit if you ever screen the film with it. Thereby invalidating your entire mix (and optical print, if you made one).

▶▶153. WHAT TO DO NOW THAT YOU REALIZE YOU SHOULD HAVE LISTENED TO THE SOUND PEOPLE.

They've realized long before you'll admit it that you have a mess on their hands. The goal is to keep them from quitting. Do what it takes. Tell them you're making yourself totally available to them, for all small and large tasks related to getting the mix together. Offer to become their assistant. Share their pain.

Here are a few things you can do to lighten their load:

- Take a Nagra or DAT recorder out and record sound effects.
- Transfer the quarter-inch or DAT tape to mag stock (if editing is on the flatbed), or digitize/transfer these to disk (if editing's on Protools).
- Listen through the endless sound-effects libraries from the thirties on and choose the effects that might work.
- Make sure the composer's coming through for you. In the meantime, find music with a beat and feeling similar enough to stand in as a "temp" track. Promise yourself not to fall in love with it, since you don't have the rights.
- Organize the Foley sessions (where hard effects such as footsteps are recorded). Volunteer to be one of the Foley artists and volunteer your friends as well.
- Shorten the scenes (through judicious picture editing) in which you'll need to get ADR.
- If the editors are working on a flatbed, offer to split the tracks as necessary (separate male and female dialogue tracks, split effects tracks for greater control in the mix, etc.).
- Offer to hand-sync the ADR dialogue to the picture.

In addition, don't neglect to: answer their calls, make their vacation arrangements, book a masseuse, or at least get a pizza delivered. Seriously, just as you budgeted for on-set crew's meals during the shoot, budget to pay for or bring in one meal a day for the deserving editors.

24

USES FOR DUCT TAPE AND OTHER QUICK FIXES

▶▶154. DUCT TAPE MIRACLES

When just ordinary tape won't do, there is duct tape or its camera department cousin, gaffer's tape. Duct tape has its cult followers, and we're two of them. Permit us to share some of its fascinating lore with you.

During World War II our nation's men in uniform needed a strong, waterproof tape to keep moisture out of ammunition cases. Since it was waterproof, it came to be referred to as "duck" tape. This versatile tape could be ripped by hand and was used to make quick repairs to military equipment like aircraft and Jeeps. After the war, the tape was used on the home front, repairing, among other things, air-ventilation systems. This is how it got the name by which we know it today: duct tape.

Here are a few of the miracle cures we've seen duct tape used for on the set:

- To lift the face of an aging actress who had to play herself twenty years younger. It really worked. At worst, she looked like she had an overzealous face-lift. She wore the duct tape to her car and out to dinner with a new date, so we knew we were on to something.
- By the wardrobe department to lift hems and to paste on sleeves where there were none. Also, to keep a fly shut on an actor's vintage pants with a rusty zipper. Yes, it required tap-

ing from the inside. Such are the joys of being a wardrobe assistant.

- By the wardrobe department to tape up an actress's sagging breasts. Such are the further joys of being a wardrobe assistant.

- To tape down just about any prop in danger of slipping, or being moved by absentminded crew. On one occasion we had an actress who was supposed to argue with her husband while holding a plate of eggs with toast. The husband ends the argument by grabbing a piece of toast off the precariously bandied-about plate. Only problem was, the toast kept slipping off before that moment. So guess what? We taped it on with a big old wad of duct tape and the scene went great— right up until the actor bit into a gob of tape and had to chew on it as if it were toast until the scene played out. But that was OK, because in addition to all of duct tape's other wondrous properties, it's nontoxic!

- Duct tape is also great for stripping the varnish off floors, so beware.

If you are starting to get the chills just thinking about the joys of duct tape, feel free to join others like you who (literally) worship the stuff. There are a *number* of websites dedicated to the varieties of duct tape and the people who love them. Check out our favorite, "The Duct Tape guys" at www.ducttapeguys.com, where you can read what the site's own "Duct Tape Mystics" predict for the future and try to "Stump the Duct Tape Guy." Carpe Ductum!

25

DON'T LEAVE THE SET WITHOUT IT

▶▶155. WHEN IT'S A WRAP

It's not when you've nailed every shot you wanted, or when you finally got that kid to cry on cue. It's at the point of diminishing returns—the one that your bank account can make quite clear.

At that point, decide which situation you're in:

1. You've shot more or less the film you thought you would, except for that one additional shot of the car chase you think you need. Close your eyes and think back to what inspired the film in the first place. What was the single moment, the specific feeling you cared about? Do you have the image that can tell it? Get that one instead of another car-chase cutaway. Then stop.

2. You've shot something essentially foreign to you. You actually don't know what's there. Meaning you also really don't know what's *not* there. Stop right here and find out what film you might have. The beauty of the camera is that it captures life. If you got any sequence of lifelike moments on camera, then you got some sort of a film. Maybe a short one. Maybe just the trailer for the film you thought you were making. Maybe a short bit featuring your film's Rosencrantz and Guildenstern rather than your lead. Maybe a comedy

when you thought you were making a drama. But maybe the only film you can get out of this material for now. Make that film. If it ends up a terrific five-minute film that could play well at festivals, you may walk away smelling like a genius.

26

DON'T WAIT UNTIL THE MIX TO FIX IT

▶▶156. SEDUCE THE EDITOR IF YOU HAVE TO: A RECIPE FOR BRIBERY.

Conflict in the editing room? Editor being a little less than flexible? Maybe it's time to use a seduction tactic to soften him or her up. We know you know the one we're talking about. You may have used it on others in the past or had it used on you. It's one of the only legal forms of workplace seduction still widely practiced by both men and women. It can be enjoyed together or alone, in the dark or out in the open. It is: the freshly baked chocolate chip cookie.

As in all matters of love and war, one must choose the weapon to suit the opponent. When attempting to seduce industry types, it is best to choose an industry cookie. In L.A. the consummate film industry bakery for both studio and indie types is The La Brea Bakery—run by baking diva extraordinaire Nancy Silverton. Nancy is not sure how many Hollywood films she's been responsible for getting to picture lock over the years, but one thing is sure—those industry gift baskets keep streaming out the door by the assistant armful.

Here's a bit of the proven magic to use on any less than cooperative editor:

1½ cups walnut halves
8 oz. bittersweet chocolate
¾ cup light brown sugar

1 cup granulated sugar
2½ sticks unsalted butter
2½ cups unbleached pastry flour

| 1 extra large egg | ½ tsp. baking soda |
| 1 tsp. pure vanilla extract | ½ tsp. baking powder |

1. Toast the walnuts for 5–6 minutes at 325 degrees, then chop coarsely.

2. Chop the chocolate into ¾-in. "chips."

3. Try not to think of your editor as you do steps 1 and 2.

4. Cream butter and sugars together.

5. Mix egg and vanilla in separate bowl, then add to creamed butter.

6. Mix dry ingredients, then add gradually to creamed butter.

7. Mix nuts and chocolate into creamed butter.

8. Gather dough into ball, wrap in plastic, and refrigerate 2 hours until firm.

9. Go back into the editing bay to see if there has been any progress while you were gone.

10. Preheat the oven to 350 degrees.

11. Form dough into 1½-in. balls, placed 2 in. apart on a parchment-lined baking sheet.

12. Flatten balls slightly with the palm of your hand.

13. Bake for 15–20 minutes rotating baking sheet midway, if possible, to promote even baking.

14. Remove cookies from oven and place on plate small enough to require you to stack cookies in a tall pyramid to get them all on the plate.

15. Return to editing bay with your weapons.

16. Eat cookies together in darkroom.

17. Experience and praise your marvelous-ness together, thereby achieving consensus on something for the first time in weeks.

18. Move on to talking about more difficult topics, like that shot sequence you want back in, as you work your way down the pile.

19. When editor asks for more cookie therapy later, and he will, give an enigmatic look and withhold a response until you get full compliance.

20. Repeat steps one through 18 until final mix, if necessary.

(recipe used by permission of Nancy Silverton—with some adaptation by Landau and White—from *The Food of Campinile*, Villard, 1997)

27

POINT(ER)S OF DISTRIBUTION

▶▶ 157. DO-IT-YOURSELF DISTRIBUTION: THE LAST RESORT.

While we make the point that other people's money can get in the way of your artistic control when you're making your film, there's nothing wrong with their money bankrolling its marketing and distribution once it's finished.

Distributing the film yourself is technically possible. You don't have to be an "official" distributor to get your film into theaters. But taking on this project means that instead of making films, you'll spend the next two years booking one screen at a time, negotiating profit sharing with the theaters or simply paying them for the service of screening it, designing and paying for the ads, persuading journalists to give you a review, paying for more prints of the film, shipping the prints to the theaters, and hoping they come back in one piece in time to send to the next theater. Then, unless you can send out your uncle Vinnie to stand by when receipts are counted, you can expect to collect only some part of the pittance you'll be owed.

Established distributors have every advantage that you don't. Strong contacts, prior history with the exhibitors, and budgets for national media campaigns help them book the right theaters for the film, and keep the film playing there for more than one weekend. Marketing and art departments let them target the audience with trailers, ads, posters, postcards, website tie-ins, and promotional events. Leverage (based on the future films they'll be outputting to exhibitors) and lawyers help get them their fair share of the receipts back.

Unless you're a special sort of iconoclast, you'll want a distributor to pick up your film. The competition to get one is where things tend to get depressing. Too many films ÷ too small a paying audience for non-Hollywood films = too few successful independent distributors = a ferocious competition to get their attention = the hell that is Sundance.

Even if you don't believe that the odds apply to you (and no one does), the fact is that most films don't get distribution. Which is why we wish you would only make films that take only as much out of you (emotionally and financially) as you can stand to lose. The main reason filmmakers try to sell their films is so they can get enough money and credibility to go back to square one and start making another film. Remember that if you make films you can afford, you can afford to make more films.

Filmmakers' strategy for getting the attention of a distributor often amounts to throwing their film at festivals and following it around to the odd towns it screens in. Accompanying your film to festivals has its folksy charm, and you might make friends and fans around the country. But if your aim is to sell your film, showing it at festivals that do not attract buyers can be a waste of time and money.

Buyers can go to only so many festivals. The herd mentality means they'll go only to the festivals where their competitors go. You won't be any closer to selling your film to buyers by screening it in Duluth than if you screened it against your kitchen wall. Why did the buyers settle on Sundance, Cannes, Toronto, and Berlin? It's a moot point. They're there. The list of "premiere" festivals evolves, and we're not attempting to be definitive by citing these perennial four. Read the trades for the latest updates on where the buyers are buying, or call up the very companies you want to have bidding over you and ask what festivals their acquisitions people will be covering this year. Logically, you would submit your film to these festivals. And, quite possibly, only to these. Since the better festivals insist that your film screen as a world premiere, showing it at smaller festivals first may actually constitute a liability.

The irony is that the very same buyers who schlep out to Sundance and Toronto in the winter are in L.A. or N.Y. the rest of the time. You don't have to go to festivals to stalk them. You could invite them to a screening close to their office, or send them a videotape to take home. One reason why they may ignore you is that your efforts at persuasion do not carry the same third-party validation that festival selection committees and audiences can bestow.

Enter the producer's rep and the publicist. Independently and together, they can give your film a professional presentation, a third-party stamp of approval, and an elusive aura of desirability vis-à-vis buyers. Particularly the good ones: whose taste is selective and whose approach is sophisticated and polite. By agreeing to represent your film, the better publicists and producer's reps can lend an authority that, coupled with their steady persistence with buyers, can help your film get seen, and seen in the best light. Whether at festivals or for screenings they organize for the buyers at home, they can work on getting the the buyers to show up and the overloaded press to notice your film. Assuming your film gets offers, your producer's rep will negotiate them on your behalf.

Laura Kim, a publicist at L.A.'s mPRm (a bicoastal public relations and producer's representation company handling film and newmedia), is so admired that reviewers we've talked to say they'll go to see a film just because she personally asked them to. *The Cruise*, a black-and-white video documentary about a New York Gray Line tour operator, didn't get into Sundance, and its filmmaker, Bennett Miller, wondered what do next. Laura agreed that the subject didn't sound very commercial on paper. But it was one of the most remarkable films she had ever seen. She represented it on nothing more than faith. She and one of the film's producers called buyers and talked with them until they understood how much it meant to her that they see it. They saw it. It sold. It got rave reviews.

Filmmakers typically hire producer's reps and publicists once they've gotten into festivals. Indeed, given the level of competition, you will be at a disadvantage without such a team at your side. The savviest filmmakers get producer's reps and publicists involved as strategic marketing consultants even before applying to festivals, to help decide which festivals to apply to, and indeed to help decide whether festivals, versus private buyers' screenings, are the best venue for the film.

After staying up later than usual, drinking more than usual, and waking up earlier than usual with coffee that's stronger than their usual, buyers and press at festivals aren't necessarily in their best frame of mind. Festivals' live audiences can work in a film's favor, particularly with comedies, which are rarely funny when watched alone or in a room of grumpy buyers. But just as easily live audiences can also work against a film. There's nothing like a bomb at Sundance to kill buyers' fever. Reviewers are another wild card. The review a film gets from the *New York Times* critic sent to cover the New York festivals will be the last one it gets from that paper. If it's bad, the film suffers a serious blow, since independent films' chances (at least in buyers' eyes) can be made or broken by the *New York Times* review.

Find the names of producer's reps and publicists through independent filmmaking support organizations such as the Independent Feature Project (IFP). Then just call them. Unlike agents, you don't need to be introduced or come with special credentials. You just need a cut of your film to send them. They'll watch it, and you'll talk.

How much money you'll spend working with producer's reps and publicists depends on standard costs in the city they work in, your budget, the scale on which you require their involvement, and on how much they love your film. It's something you'll negotiate case by case. We know of cases where these professionals worked on a deferred-pay basis (i.e., essentially free) because they couldn't help themselves. The film's beauty and significance made them do it.

▶▶ 158. YOU TRIED, AND YOU DIDN'T GET A DISTRIBUTOR.

At this point it's time to get really honest about your goals, and realistic about what constitutes meeting them.

Are you trying to get money back?

The money you'll spend on prints and ads to get a paying audience can put you further in the hole. Especially when you consider that studios typically spend the equivalent of a production budget on marketing a film. P.S.: a full-page ad in N.Y. and L.A. papers starts at $40,000.

Are you still trying to get a distributor?

Recognize that it's a real long shot to get your film "noticed" by distributors who have already have seen it and passed. If you haven't already, now's the time to work with a publicist and producer's rep who can help you come up with the strategy you may have missed. One strategy that doesn't work: opening the film yourself in L.A. or N.Y. in order to give buyers a chance to see it. These major markets are your film's best chances at revenue. By opening your film yourself in these markets, you're "stealing" these receipts away from the potential distributors of the film, making them less likely to buy it.

Are you trying to get an audience?

With more festivals nationwide than independent art screens, it's time to recognize festivals as a distribution route. You can piece together a national audience through college screens and festivals. Then there's the power of TV, including cable. The Sundance Channel, with six million subscriber homes, can get your film to a larger audience than theaters ever hope to. Among the Internet's many wonders is that it's a free distribution outlet for your film, open to any and all audiences you can point there, 24/7.

Are you trying to get closure?

Closure is important. Maybe most of all vis-à-vis your investors. You can buy yourself a N.Y. or L.A. premiere—at an amazingly reasonable price. For just $500 you can book morning or midnight shows for a weekend at L.A.'s prestigious Nu Art and Laemmle's art house theaters. Work ahead of time with the theaters' gentle-hearted staffs, and you can even get coverage in the their published calendars, distributed to thousands of local film addicts. They might even be able to help you get reviewers to show up, particularly if they love your film. Real, live, paying theatergoers might actually come to your movie. In addition to your friends, family, investors, and agent, and anyone else to whom you owe an explanation or a thank-you.

▶▶159. WHAT YOU'LL ABSOLUTELY NEED, WHETHER YOU WORK WITH A DISTRIBUTOR, A PUBLICIST, OR NOT.

- Good production stills from your film. You can't turn back time and get these once your film wraps. There's no substitute for them, and you can never have enough, so get, at the very least, the basics: clear, compelling images of your main cast in singles, your main cast in doubles (representing the main relationships in the film), and some shots of you and your crew making the film. For reproduction in ads and festival brochures you'll need black-and-white prints and color slides. Color prints are useless. Attempting to blow up stills from the film's print is truly a matter of last resort: they end up looking muddy and terrible.

- Copies of an up-to-date press kit. The kit should include: basic specs (year made, running time, format, genre, locations used, legal representation or producer's rep if applicable), stills (at least two from the film and one of the director), a one-page synopsis, a one-line synopsis, complete list of cast and their characters, bios of your cast and principal crew, the director's filmography, production notes (i.e., the story of how the film came about and was made), reviews/press and list of awards as you accumulate them (keep the best, winnow out the rest—don't make your kit cross the line into a sentimental scrapbook), and contact information. Especially when soliciting press attention, contact phone and fax numbers and e-mail should have a live person on the other end, or check messages regularly. Reporters work under deadlines, and returning a call after the press run means you blew your chance. Use simple pocket folders for presentation, since they let you add and remove documents. Keep materials neat, and design clear and consistent. Limit your use of fonts, and use the same title fonts used in the film's credits to reinforce the film's visual "brand."

- A good title for the film. This is the first and perhaps single most significant marketing decision you can make for your film. Private jokes don't play. The title should capture the spirit of what the film has to offer to an audience.

- A reasonable supply of videotapes of your film ready to send out at a moment's notice. You don't want to have to make excuses that they're still being dubbed (i.e., that you still need to find money to make dubs), especially after you've worked so hard to get to this point. Make sure, however, that the tapes you are sending out are copy protected!

- Posters to paper the town with when your film plays in festivals. Leave blank space at the bottom to write in where and when the film's playing, so you can use the posters in a variety of venues.

- A strong sense of your film's audience and the willingness to go after them by any means necessary. If your film has a natural, self-identified audience (around a specific passion, cause, ethnicity, sexuality, spirituality, gender, life experience, etc.), you will need to capture its interest and harness its word-of-mouth support before you can hope to build a broader "crossover" audience. Build awareness in your natural audience through its own channels, including meetings, conventions, restaurants, cafés and hangouts, film festivals, neighborhoods, newspapers. Don't neglect to arrange special free screenings for these critical ambassadors.

- Respect for the importance of word of mouth. Liz Manne, executive vice president of Programming and Marketing at Sundance Channel, used to be head of marketing for Fine Line Features, and was responsible for the extraordinary campaigns for *Hoop Dreams* and *Shine*. She based her marketing strategy on a grid she drew to identify a film's relative marketability and playability. A film with high marketability has recognizable elements that help presell it easily: movie stars, high-concept story line (easily summed up in the title: e.g., *Twins* with Schwarzenegger and DeVito, *Titanic, Star Wars*), high-concept sales hook (*The Blair Witch Project*, "made" by the actor/filmmakers who have since "disappeared"), amazing special effects, clear genre. Generally, independent films are weak in these categories and need to shoot for high "playability"—meaning that they need to please audiences who get to see the film. Marketing for these films depends more on the long-term power of word-of-mouth marketing than advance hype. To orchestrate word-of-mouth marketing for films such as *Shine*, Fine Line arranged free screenings for groups of people who spend all day talking to other people, including hairdressers, teachers, and retail salespeople. Do anything you can to get the talkers talking about your film, as long as you're confident they'll say good things.
- Maturity to recognize that the money you spent on your film is unrelated to what people will spend to see it or to distribute it. Even if you spent $1 million on your film, if people will not spend money to see it, then your film is, in pure commercial terms, worth $0. Accept and respect the revenues the market (and by extension, the distributors) will bear.

28

ONE OR TWO MORE THINGS BEFORE THE LIGHTS COME UP

▶▶160. SACRIFICE ANYTHING TO CLARITY.

You can't pass out Cliffs Notes or study guides to your film with the popcorn. You won't be able to stand in front of an audience before and after every screening explaining what went wrong and what everything was really supposed to mean.

Make the story clear so that the audience can get on with enjoying the film. They won't be talking about that amazing push-in, pull-out dolly shot pan if they're trying to figure out what happened.

The story is the spine through which your characters can move and experience change. Likewise, it's the route through which your audience can go through an experience. It's the ski-lift butt bar they hold onto. Pull it out from under them, and they're left to careen down icy mountains on their backs and land on their face.

You may counter that thrillers and mysteries work with the element of withholding. Look closer. Thrillers actually get their spine chills by letting you know something the protagonist doesn't so that you can worry about it on their behalf. Mysteries pay off only if every step the detective takes to solve them is clear and rational.

Your film is a haikulike condensation of life. By convention, the audience expects everything you put into it to matter. If it doesn't work to advance the story or deepen the characters, take it out. It will only confuse the view and tire the audience, demanding that they care about things that don't matter. Leave in unnecessary material—an inside joke that no one understands, or a shot of your girlfriend that no one else cares about—and you've made a mistake people call "indulgence." If you're not serving the audience, the only other person you must be serving is yourself.

▶▶161. ANY FILM THAT MAKES THEM CRY IS A GOOD FILM

They're crying? Don't change a thing. They'll love you for it or hate you for it, but they'll remember the film. You've given them an emotional experience, which will count in the repertoire of their life experiences. It's like giving someone a memory of something that has never happened to them personally but felt that way. There is a tremendous amount of responsibility that goes along with this.

An experience is an experience—the unconscious can't tell the difference. The tears are a sign of authentic experience, and the sign that you've just affected someone's life. Tears are the result of the audience's empathy with the characters and ideas in your film. They reveal that the audience has felt the character's struggle, and felt it as their own. Could you ask for anything more?

You've touched on the real power of film. The profound power to guide an audience to feel someone else's life as if it were their own. Imagine the humanist, not to mention psychedelic possibilities: you can make southern white men feel like northern black women, today's teenagers feel like twelfth-century monks, Californians feel like ethnic Albanians, us feel like Shelley Long or Dolly Parton. You can put an audience into someone else's skin, forgetting their own problems for the sake of the character's. It's a radical, magical tool, and if you've learned how to use it, or stumbled on to the power, protect and value it like a spell Merlin slipped you.

29

DO IT AGAIN

If you want to make films, make films.